## What Readers Are Saying About
### *The Dream Team Nightmare*

Engaging and fun to read, the *Dream Team Nightmare* is jam-packed with fresh ideas and techniques that are easy to adopt. It's also a great springboard for follow-up reading on the bigger ideas, such as systems thinking. I would heartily recommend it to everyone to share with their teams.

➤ **Victoria Morgan-Smith, Scrum master**

*The Dream Team Nightmare* is a breath of fresh air in comparison to other books out there on project theory and process. It provides you with a wealth of information to make better decisions on your project.

➤ **James Major, project manager, Network Rail**

*The Dream Team Nightmare* is a crash course in Agile. I strongly recommend it to all readers involved in building software products, from technical to product people.

➤ **Dyan Corutiu, software developer**

*The Dream Team Nightmare* is an innovative and entertaining read that helped me learn some new ideas and techniques, had me thinking about how I work, and kept me wanting to continue the adventure.

➤ **Karl Scotland, agile coach, Rally Software**

*The Dream Team Nightmare* is packed with tips and concrete techniques for how to do just about everything an agile coach does. Portia's entertaining book is totally unlike any other agile book you've ever read.

➤ **Liz Sedley, author of *Agile Coaching***

This is the most fun read I've had in a long time. I anticipate that it will have the same dramatic effect for agile methods as *The Goal* did for systems thinking. You should read it at least twice: once for enjoyment and a second time for deeper learning.

➤ **Matt Gelbwaks, transformation coach, North Main LLC**

*The Dream Team Nightmare* shows in a gentle-yet-concrete way how an Agile coach works. A great book for anyone working to introduce agile to others.

➤ **Michael McCullough, founder of Tastycupcakes.org, executive technical director at Quadrus Development**

The game of life is to try, learn, and adapt through small and frequent experiments. The palette of problems and creative solutions will surprise experienced agile practitioners as well as new enthusiasts.

➤ **Staffan Nöteberg, author of *Pomodoro Technique Illustrated***

# The Dream Team Nightmare

Boost Team Productivity Using Agile Techniques

Portia Tung

The Pragmatic Bookshelf

Dallas, Texas • Raleigh, North Carolina

Many of the designations used by manufacturers and sellers to distinguish their products are claimed as trademarks. Where those designations appear in this book, and The Pragmatic Programmers, LLC was aware of a trademark claim, the designations have been printed in initial capital letters or in all capitals. The Pragmatic Starter Kit, The Pragmatic Programmer, Pragmatic Programming, Pragmatic Bookshelf, PragProg and the linking *g* device are trademarks of The Pragmatic Programmers, LLC.

Every precaution was taken in the preparation of this book. However, the publisher assumes no responsibility for errors or omissions, or for damages that may result from the use of information (including program listings) contained herein.

Our Pragmatic courses, workshops, and other products can help you and your team create better software and have more fun. For more information, as well as the latest Pragmatic titles, please visit us at *http://pragprog.com*.

The team that produced this book includes:

Lynn Beighley (editor)
Molly McBeath (copyeditor)
David J Kelly (typesetter)
Janet Furlow (producer)
Juliet Benda (rights)
Ellie Callahan (support)

Printed in the United States of America.
ISBN-13: 978-1-937785-71-0
Printed on acid-free paper.
Book version: P1.0—December 2013

*To Snow Dragon*

*For making dreams come true*

# Contents

# Acknowledgments

The colorful story of *The Dream Team Nightmare* has come to life thanks to all the people and teams I've worked with and learned from in the past decade.

Special thanks to everyone who has encouraged me to have fun and keep writing, including Michael McCullough, Paul Field, Staffan Nöteberg, Özlem Yuce, Matt Gelbwaks, Liz Sedley, Lesley Rantell Seldon, Karl Scotland, Jenni Jepsen, James Major, Carsten Ruseng Jakobsen, Ben Seldon, Carolyn Donovan, Claire Hannon, Victoria Morgan-Smith, Graham Lee, Filippo Macchiettini, Antti Kirjavainen, David Peterson, Dan Talpău, Monika Koscian, Steve Hollings, Thorsten Kalnin, Alissa Fingleton, Maria Bortes, Dyan Corutiu, Tamas Jano, Ioana Jano, Chris Hogben, Kate Newdigate, Simon Parkinson, Sandro Mancuso, Pete Thomas, Mazda Hewitt, Vera Peeters, Pascal Van Cauwenberghe, Jenni Jepsen, Yves Hanoulle, Steve Holyer, Derek Graham, Clarke Ching, Phil Trelford, Markku Ahman, Kevlin Henney, Olaf Lewitz, Pat Kua, Eoin Woods, Simon Brown, Nat Pryce, Jens Hoffmann, Benjamin Tung, Linda Yung, Bill Tung, Annie Luk, Chantal Ellam, Sara Lewis, Sharmila Sabaratnam, Steven Smith, and Chris Bird. Thank you also for your endless gifts of feedback.

Last, but not least, many thanks to the Pragmatic Bookshelf team for introducing me to the art of publishing.

# Preface

Welcome to *The Dream Team Nightmare*, an agile adventure. As an agile adventurer, you'll meet a whole host of characters in lots of different scenarios. You'll be faced with many challenges, and your success will depend on the quality of the decisions you make.

During this agile adventure, you get to decide what to do. Once you've made your choice, turn to the corresponding section to find out what happens next. Keep reading until you have to make your next decision. Repeat these steps until you reach the end of your adventure.

Each adventure is a test of your skills, knowledge, and experience. Unlike in the real world, if at first you don't succeed, you can start all over again.

They say luck is when opportunity meets preparation. Be prepared and good luck!

# How to Use This Book

Before setting off on this agile adventure...

If you're new to agile or want to learn more about the basics of agile, I suggest first reading one or both of the following books:

- *The Scrum Guide* by Jeff Sutherland and Ken Schwaber (16 pages). This can be downloaded for free from:

  https://www.scrum.org/Scrum-Guides

- *Scrum and XP from the Trenches* by Henrik Kniberg (130 pages). This is also a free download from:

  http://www.infoq.com/minibooks/scrum-xp-from-the-trenches

If you've worked on one or more agile projects, then jump right in. As you read the book, you may find unfamiliar terms and concepts. You'll find definitions for these in the glossary toward the end of the book. If you find there's a lot of unfamiliar terminology, I suggest you take a break to read *The Scrum Guide* to make your journey more enjoyable.

Begin the adventure on page 2.

# Part I

# Begin the Adventure

# About You

Your name is Jim Hopper. You've worked with a dozen agile teams in the past three years. You've typically worked as an agile coach-consultant hired by companies at the start of their agile journey. Of the teams you've coached, six have continued to flourish long after you left, while others have stagnated. You found out last week that the most recent of the teams you've coached has abandoned agile altogether and returned to waterfall in order to meet a deadline.

Your background is diverse. You began working as a software developer in the dot-com boom coding in Java. Then you moved on to coding in .NET. You came across agile through XP (which is short for extreme programming). After five years as a software developer, you became a development manager and tried to introduce Scrum into an organization with limited success.

Eventually, you learned how to increase business agility by implementing a hybrid of agile methods (such as XP, Scrum, and Kanban) and lean.

You haven't written production code for almost a decade, so you can't claim to be a developer anymore. However, having been a software developer has given you practical insight into the complex nature of software development.

Specializing in organizational change through people and process improvement is hard work. Given the ups and downs of your agile coaching track record, your reputation is now at stake. The outcome of your latest engagement will determine if you stick with agile coaching or give up doing what you love.

Your CV is available on LinkedIn on page 265.

Continue with the adventure on page 3.

# Meet Your Team

Today is your first day at Love Inc., an award-winning online dating business. You've just been introduced to your new team as their agile coach.

"We call ourselves the 'Dream Team,'" begins Ben, the team lead, as he shakes your hand. "Most of us come from a waterfall background. We've been experimenting with the agile methodology for the past eighteen months and things just don't seem to be working out."

"What specific challenges is the team facing?" you ask the group.

"We've been wasting our time on getting the team to collaborate instead of building our product," blurts out Jason, one of the developers.

"We run around like headless chickens," says Matt, another developer. "I've been with the company since it started and I've never seen so little progress in such a long time."

"Does anyone actually know where we are on the project plan?" asks William, another developer. "By my count, we haven't shipped any software for at least the past three months."

Most people shake their heads, while others groan and shift in their chairs.

"One of our biggest problems is the large number of issues raised by the business," says Nancy, the tester. "We spend a lot of time debating if an issue is a defect or a change in requirement."

"Discussions about issues with the business always end in an argument," adds William.

"The result is that we now have a reputation for producing the worst-quality software the business has ever seen," says Ben.

"What would the business people say if they were here?" you ask.

Another developer, Roger, replies. "I know exactly what Cassandra, our product owner, would say." Roger does what can only be an impression of Cassandra as he places both hands on his hips and says in a suddenly high-pitched voice, "The team makes up requirements that nobody wants."

Roger relaxes, then mutters, "Personally, I can't believe that customers wouldn't find that funky widget we came up with useful. It uses the latest front-to-back web technology stack."

Ben continues. "Our reply to the business would be, 'If only you can tell us exactly what you want, we would build it for you.'" Ben shakes his head. "All we need is for the business people to stop changing their minds every five seconds," he adds.

"So how long have you got to help us sort out our problems?" asks Matt as everyone turns toward you.

You remain silent for a moment. "The management has given us five days to come up with an action plan to get things moving forward again," you say.

Do you:

- continue with the adventure on page 5,
- first review a confidential company report compiled by an external consultant on page 230, or
- review the email describing the goals of your mission at Love Inc. on page 236?

# Go for Broke

The Dream Team's situation is familiar. You've worked with a number of teams over the years and you recognize the deterioration in performance as part of the seasonal life cycle of teams.

Based on what you already know about the team and your past experience, you could not only formulate a plan but roll it out immediately to get the project back on track.

Or you could choose to wait in order to gather more information about the current situation. You would do this by observing and working with the team before co-creating a plan of action.

You know that whatever you choose to do could make or break your relationship with the team and impact the success of this engagement.

Do you:

- push forward with your own plan on page 232, or
- gather more information first on page 8?

## Dire Straits

You like and respect Patrick. He's direct and up-front. He's also the main reason you accepted the job.

"How long have you been here, Jim?" asks Patrick. Without waiting for an answer, Patrick tells you he's received serious complaints from members of the Dream Team.

"A couple of people have reported that you tried to bully them during a team meeting. There was mention of you striking the table with your fist in anger, with possible threat of further violence," says Patrick. "Others have expressed concern over your credentials because your behavior during that meeting has shown them you talk a good talk about agile, but you fail to lead by example."

Patrick continues. "I know that we're a dysfunctional organization and change would never be easy. I've spoken to the other managers and we agree that the Dream Team isn't the right fit for you after all."

Do you:

- defend yourself against the allegations on page 241, or
- wait to hear what else Patrick has to say on page 7?

# One More Chance

Patrick tells you they'll be hiring someone else to help the Dream Team.

You remain silent for a moment. You realize that by pushing forward with your own agenda instead of listening to the team, you've alienated everyone that matters. What's more, it has cost you their trust, something you're unlikely to regain no matter how hard you try.

Nonetheless, Patrick believes you have the potential to add value to the company. He offers you a second chance. Patrick asks you to switch teams and coach the Green Team instead.

This isn't the first time you've been asked to switch teams. It's happened a couple of times before under similar circumstances. Something has to change or else you're likely to fail again. The key is to start applying the agile values and principles to the way you behave, not just to how you manage the work. The secret lies in walking the walk, not just talking the talk, as you well know.

You accept Patrick's offer and walk out of his office ready for a different adventure.

THE END

## Time to Talk

Having worked on projects with responsibilities spanning the entire software development life cycle from analysis to project management to production support, you've come to realize that the biggest challenge in software development isn't technology. That's because although technology is forever evolving, people always figure out how to solve technology problems—sooner or later.

The real challenge lies with people, a factor common to all projects. In your experience, it's also one of the key factors that determines the likelihood of success. That's why you choose to invest time from the outset in getting to know the people you work with. You understand that people are a company's greatest asset and that effective teamwork is a prerequisite for releasing business value now and in the future.

It's time to get to know each team member through a thirty-minute conversation, one on one.

Continue with the adventure on page 9.

# Get to Know the Team

Before meeting individually with the team members, you prepare an agenda to get the most value from each one-on-one conversation. You take out a pack of mini sticky notes. You always carry some because they always come in handy.

First, you write out the three headings that give your plan a structure, one per sticky note.

- *To Do*
- *In Progress*
- *Done*

Next, you write out each of the following topics, one per sticky note. The sticky notes form the proposed conversation plan. They also serve as a reminder of the topics to be covered, as well as enable you to keep track of progress during the meeting.

- *Ice Breaker*
- *Professional Background*
- *Agile Experience*
- *3 Wishes*
- *???*

You take this opportunity to mentally rehearse what's covered in each topic.

ICE BREAKER

You like to begin with a game. The idea is to take turns asking each other questions, with a total of three questions each. The only rule is that each person reserves the right to ask for a different question. Your personal favorites include the following:

1. "If you could do anything in the entire world other than your current job, what would it be?"
2. "What do you spend most of your spare time doing?"
3. "What's your favorite holiday destination?"

PROFESSIONAL BACKGROUND

In this section, the two of you exchange work histories leading up to your respective current roles.

AGILE EXPERIENCE

Here you ask the other person to tell you about his or her level and amount of experience in agile. You will have usually talked about your agile experience when you discussed your professional background.

3 WISHES

You like to finish off with another game. You ask the other person, "If you could have three wishes for transforming your daily work and/or workplace, what would they be?"

???

This topic represents a wildcard. You include this so that the other person can propose any topics he or she would like to discuss.

Continue with the adventure on page 11.

# Dialogue

You always begin each conversation by thanking team members up front for their time. Then you go through the proposed conversation plan together.

First you lay out the three heading sticky notes side-by-side: To Do, In Progress, Done. Then you lay out each topic sticky note, one at a time, under the To Do heading. When you reach the sticky note that reads "???" (wildcard), you ask the team member if there are any topics he or she would like to talk about during this session. This ensures you both get something out of the meeting. Then you write out his or her topics, one per sticky note. You discard the "???" sticky note and lay out the new suggestions in its place.

It's at this point that you and the team member come up with the final version of the conversation plan on the understanding that you'll both review and replan based on what's most valuable and necessary to cover during the meeting. You offer the option to arrange a follow-up meeting to discuss any outstanding topics.

As the conversation progresses, you both agree on the next step before moving a sticky note from To Do, to In Progress, and finally to Done. You make sure the two of you can always see and move the sticky notes around, as the meeting involves you both.

If you have a spare moment at the end, you like to ask the team member for feedback on how he or she thinks the session went. You always end each conversation as you started, thanking the team member for spending time with you.

Given that it's an informal conversation, you seldom make notes during this meeting. Instead you jot down your thoughts afterward. This helps put you both at ease, as well as gives you the chance to practice your listening skills.

Continue with the adventure on page 18.

# Coach Notes from Team One-on-Ones

After meeting with a few more team members, you jot down some notes.

Nancy — tester

- "Agile soap opera"; 18 mths ago, quality at all-time low
- Gave agile a go, produced "best software the company's ever seen"
- Now back to producing defects instead of software that people enjoy using

Jason — developer

- "Expert in agile; been there, done that, bought the T-shirt"
- "Most senior developer in team"
- First team at Love Inc. to adopt agile
- "Methodologies are fads and don't change a thing."

Ben — Scrum master

- Team rushed through agile basics
- Didn't build on strong foundation of knowledge and experience
- Some team members call themselves "agile experts."
- Not everyone wants to improve
- Things got worse; team abandoned agile three months ago

Roger — developer

- First job; hired to be on an agile team
- "Agile's a natural way of working for me."
- Started off as a team, egos got in the way, daily scrums took too long
- Nothing improved in spite of retrospectives

- Some team members call themselves "agile experts" — the 'do as we say, not as we do' kind.

Rebecca — business analyst

- Historically, a bad track record between the business and IT when the two groups should have been working as one

- Agile improved relationships and software quality; releases every two weeks

- People got complacent, stopped practicing agile

- Quality now worse than ever before; threat of project being outsourced

- Wonders if she should start looking for another job

Continue with the adventure on page 14.

## Working Lunch

This morning, you've met with five of the team members. On the list are four more developers and the product owner.

It's time for a break. When you return to the team space, you casually inquire what people do for lunch around here. Social rituals tell you a lot about a group and about a company's culture.

"A few of us usually have lunch together," Matt tells you. "You're welcome to join us."

Do you:

- have lunch with the team on page 15, or
- explore the vicinity on your own on page 17?

# Read Between the Lines

You walk over to the cafeteria with Matt, the developer who coarchitected the framework with Jason on which the software product is built.

"It's good to have you here. We've needed fresh blood for a while. Roger's great because he says what's on his mind, and he's usually right. The problem is that he doesn't have seniority within the team, so most of his suggestions get ignored."

Nancy, Ben, Rebecca, and Ash (another developer on the team) are eating their lunch by the time the two of you arrive.

"Where's Roger?" you ask.

"Roger and William go to the gym every lunchtime," says Ash.

"Roger wants to be beach-ready," Nancy adds. It's February, and everyone laughs, including you.

"And what about the others?" you ask.

"Ethan goes running by the river on Mondays, Wednesdays, and Thursdays," says Ben.

"Jason never has lunch with the rest of the team," says Matt. "We've tried inviting him a couple of times, but he prefers to eat and work alone."

It feels like you're beginning to get to know the team. After lunch, you buy a cup of coffee and some cookies for later.

Continue with the adventure on page 16.

## More Team One-on-Ones

In the afternoon, you have your one-on-ones with the other four team members. It seems that everyone has a similar story to tell. At the end of your conversation with Ethan, he asks the question everyone else is wondering about. "Do you think you can help us turn things around?"

"Many things become possible when people choose to work together," you say.

The series of one-on-ones have been intense and invaluable. You want to speak to Cassandra, the product owner, as soon as possible, but you discover she's away on business and won't be back until next week.

Continue with the adventure on page 20.

## Time Out

You thank Matt for the lunch invitation but decline. "I'm heading out for some fresh air," you say. You can always have lunch with the team tomorrow. Meanwhile, you need time to yourself to reflect on this morning's conversations.

As you step out into the rain, you wonder where this adventure will take you. In your experience, although organizations may look very different from the outside, many of the challenges they face are, in fact, surprisingly similar. After all, as they say, "the people make the place."

The biggest challenge for you will be to keep a cool head when everyone else around you is losing theirs. You hope that all your previous experience and learning prepares you well for what lies ahead. Only time will tell.

Continue with the adventure on page 244.

## More About You

One of the reasons you enjoy having team one-on-ones is because it helps you gain new insights into people and their situations. Nancy, who's passionate about testing, surprises you with a few choice questions during the Ice Breaker section of her one-on-one with you.

"I can ask you whatever I like?" says Nancy with a big smile. You nod and she volunteers to go first. "So what's your favorite hobby?" Nancy asks.

"I run at least three times a week. I've run a few 10k races. I plan to run a marathon one day," you reply.

"Why do you run?" asks Nancy.

"Because it helps me relax and think more clearly about things."

"Any other reasons?" continues Nancy.

"It helps quiet my mind in a noisy world," you say.

It's your turn to ask Nancy a question.

"If you could do anything in the entire world other than your current job, what would it be?" you ask.

You discover that Nancy has a five-year-old daughter named Sophia, with whom she loves spending time. Nancy enjoys making up fairy tales to tell Sophia and hopes to one day write children's stories.

It's Nancy's turn. "What's one of your weaknesses?"

You have many weaknesses. You pick the one you're working on improving at the moment.

"My work comes first because I want to give 100 percent to what I do," you say. "But I end up neglecting people I care about. With practice, I hope to one day find a sustainable work-life balance."

It's your turn to ask another question. "What's your favorite movie?" you say.

Nancy smiles. "The Wizard of Oz."

"Why is it your favorite?" you continue.

"I know this sounds cheesy," says Nancy, "but the story reminds me that each of us has everything we need within ourselves to solve the problems we face. I sometimes lose sight of this after yet another day of wrestling with the madness that is our project."

You nod. "One more Ice Breaker question each," you say.

"Is there someone special in your life? I can ask something else if you like," Nancy says with a wink and smile.

"I'm seeing someone," you reply.

"Can you tell me a bit about her?" she persists.

You laugh. "I think you've used up all your questions," you reply. "What do you want to know?"

While asking the three Ice Breaker questions helps you get to know someone quickly, it's even better when the questions and answers flow like a natural conversation.

"What's her name? What does she do?" continues Nancy.

"Her name's Emily," you say. "She's a elementary school teacher. We've known each other for three months now."

"My turn," you say. You like to finish the chat on a lighthearted note, so you ask Nancy about her favorite vacation spot.

"It's got to be Finland!" says Nancy. "My husband and I went to see the northern lights for our honeymoon in Oulanka National Park, just south of the Arctic Circle. I'd love to take Sophia next time!"

Continue with the adventure on page 12.

# Information Gathering

Later on in the afternoon, after you've spoken individually with the nine available team members, you offer them each a cookie to go with their coffee.

Meanwhile, you ask people about their availability for a team meeting, a project retrospective. You explain that the meeting is a chance for everyone to share their thoughts about where the project is at and how you can all move it forward together.

You schedule the meeting for tomorrow afternoon from 2 to 4 p.m. because that's when everyone's available.

Next, you need to find out about the software product the team is building. Everyone seems very busy, so you ask for volunteers to get you up to speed.

You spend the first half of the afternoon with Rebecca, who talks you through the project scope and gives you a status update on the requirements implemented and those yet to be implemented.

After that, Ash and Roger jointly walk you through the design and implementation details.

Continue with the adventure on page 21.

# Trouble

According to Ash and Roger, some of the brand-new software components already require reengineering from scratch. You're reminded once again how a piece of software can tell you a lot about the team that built it. Judging by the way the software is rotting from the inside out, the Dream Team is dysfunctional at best.

In order to find out more about the project, you pose the following questions to Rebecca, Ash, and Roger.

Continue with the adventure on page 22.

# Project Evaluation

The questions are divided into four categories: value, cost, quality, and time. You write down their responses next to each question.

VALUE

- *Question: How is business value calculated and measured?*

  Answer: No idea.

- *Question: How accurate is estimated business value compared with actual value delivered by the project?*

  Answer: No idea.

COST

- *Question: How is effort calculated and measured?*

  Answer: Using story points—the number of points per sprint-level story is determined by the amount of effort required to deliver the story and by the complexity of the story.

- *Question: How accurate is estimated effort compared with actual effort delivered per release?*

  Answer: Very inaccurate.

- *Question: How much does it cost the business to make a release?*

  Answer: A lot—after development ends, there's a four-week regression testing period.

- *Question: How much per release do defects cost the business (such as the loss of new business but excluding the cost of remediation)?*

  Answer: We don't track that, although we probably should, now that you mention it.

QUALITY

- *Question: How many defects are there per release?*

  Answer: Less than a hundred?

- *Question: What is the cost of remediation per release?*

  Answer: Probably as much as the cost of feature development.

- *Question: How long does it take to discover a defect?*

  Answer: Depends—sometimes a week, sometimes as long as a month.

TIME

- *Question: How long does it take for a requirement to get from an idea to the end customer?*

  Answer: Quickest is eight weeks—it usually takes longer.

- *Question: How long does it take for a requirement to get from the planning stages to the end customer?*

  Answer: Quickest has been five weeks, but those were exceptions. In general, it takes one to two months.

- *How often is software released? When was the last release? And the release previous to that one?*

  Answer: Can't remember the last time we released— must be over three months ago.

Continue with the adventure on page 24.

## Relief

The key to information gathering is consistent questioning and an open mind. A common complaint among the team members is that requirements that have little to do with the project are always given top priority.

To ensure you get a balanced view, you plan to pose the same questions to Cassandra, the product owner, when she becomes available.

It's been a fruitful first day. It's almost time to go home.

Do you:

- write your daily log on page 25, or
- go for a walk to help you reflect on the day on page 26?

# Coach's Log: Day 1

February 1

ACTIVITIES

- Had one-on-one conversations with all team members (excluding the product owner)
- Scheduled project retrospective for tomorrow
- Got project scope and requirements overview from Rebecca
- Got technical design and implementation walk-through from Ash and Roger

WHAT WENT WELL

- Got to know the team members through one-on-one conversations
- Had lunch with some of the team members
- Learned a lot more about the project history, current status, and team dynamics

WHAT WENT WRONG

- Should have ensured everyone was invited to the team lunch so I could better see the team dynamics in play.
- Haven't met product owner yet

PUZZLES

- How quickly can I arrange to speak to the product owner?
- Why is there friction between Jason and the rest of the team?

IMPROVEMENT ACTIONS

- Invite Jason for lunch with the team next time.
- Ask team for more real-time input and feedback so that I can serve the team better.

DAY RATING: 8/10

Continue with the adventure on page 29.

# Walkabout

You like to explore the physical space where you work. The layout of an office, along with its furniture, can tell you as much about a company's culture as the people do.

Hidden from the usual flow of human traffic, behind a wall, is a team space covered in sticky notes. Like the Dream Team's space, each desk has a pair of monitors. However, instead of one keyboard and mouse per computer, there are two. This is a sign that the team does pair programming.

On the wall is a poster of a Predator, the creature from the film of the same name. Beside it is a group picture annotated with each team member's name and phone number.

In the middle of the wall is the team's kanban board, with a work-in-progress limit of three in the In Progress column. According to the team's burndown chart, the team is halfway through sprint 2 of their next release.

Although the team's current velocity is slightly lower than its linear burndown rate, the team has stuck to their WIP limit of three. Of the three WIP items, one is blocked by two impediments: one dated a week ago and another dated today. Someone called Aidan is responsible for taking care of both impediments.

These bits of information give you the impression of a healthy and performant team. You plan to introduce yourself to Team Predator sometime. For now, you find a quiet corner to reflect on Day 1 before heading home.

Continue with the adventure on page 27.

# Coach's Log: Day 1

February 1

ACTIVITIES

- Had one-on-one conversations with all team members (excluding the product owner)

- Scheduled project retrospective for tomorrow

- Got project scope and requirements overview from Rebecca

- Got technical design and implementation walk-through from Ash and Roger

- Discovered Team Predator's team space

WHAT WENT WELL

- Got to know the team members through one-on-one conversations

- Had lunch with some of the team members

- Learned a lot more about the project history and current status

- Began to see team dynamics in action

WHAT WENT WRONG

- Should have invited Jason to lunch with team

- Haven't met product owner yet

PUZZLES

- How quickly can I arrange to speak to the product owner?

- There seems to be a mismatch between Jason and the rest of the team—what's that about?

IMPROVEMENT ACTIONS

- Invite Jason for lunch with the team next time.

- Ask team for more real-time input and feedback so that I can serve the team better.

DAY RATING: 8/10

Continue with the adventure on page 29.

## Daily Update

Day 2 starts with a visit to Patrick, the manager who hired you. You had suggested up front that the two of you meet for fifteen minutes every day so that Patrick can track your progress. It's also an opportunity for Patrick to give you input and feedback.

Patrick agreed. He also said that at some point he'd like to invite other managers to the meeting to get them more involved. You like and respect Patrick. He's one of the reasons you accepted the job.

You begin by giving Patrick a brief update on what you did yesterday by referring to your notes in your daily personal coach log. Keeping a record of past activities is one of the reasons you keep a personal log. Another is that it helps you think about and reflect on what's happening in an engagement. Last but not least, it helps you realize when you're stuck and need help.

Next, you go through your plan for today. "We have a project retrospective from 2 to 4 p.m. today," you say. You explain the immediate goal is to surface the issues surrounding the communication gap between the team members. Only then can the team start addressing the other issues in priority order.

Patrick tells you he'd like to attend the project retrospective.

Do you:

- think it's a bad idea on page 30,
- think it's a good idea on page 32, or
- postpone making the decision on page 33?

## Safety First

On this occasion, you think it's a bad idea to have Patrick present during the project retrospective. To get the most value from the exercise, it's important to create an open and safe environment, where team members feel free to share their concerns and air their grievances without fear of repercussions. What's more, this is a crucial opportunity for you and the team to develop a relationship of trust.

You share these reasons with Patrick and he agrees that it's best to limit the meeting to only team members this time.

"I'd be interested in seeing the output," says Patrick, "with the team's permission of course."

"I'll be sure to ask the team," you say.

You know that if the team members agree, you could ensure confidentiality by typing up the information gathered if people are worried their comments can be traced back to them through their handwriting. There are many ways to share information effectively and safely.

Continue with the adventure on page 31.

# Here Be Dragons

Last, but not least, you tell Patrick there are no blockers that prevent you from immediately making further progress.

Patrick says, "Jim, let me know as soon as you need anything." He warns you that it's not the first time they've gotten someone in to help the Dream Team. In most cases, it has only made matters worse.

Patrick adds, "We really appreciate your help. Happily Ever After is our flagship product, and the last thing we want to do is outsource our crown jewel. Unless we have to."

As you get up to leave, Patrick shakes your hand.

Before you know it, you're standing in the corridor, faced with a challenging day ahead.

Continue with the adventure on page 34.

## Kowtow

Since Patrick's asked to attend, you feel obliged to say yes. After all, isn't the customer always right? In any case, you don't see the harm in having Patrick present at the project retrospective, so long as he remains an observer. What's more, this would be a good opportunity for Patrick to see you in action.

Yet you feel a knot in your stomach. If Patrick's presence at the project retrospective seems like such a great idea, why does your gut disagree?

Nonetheless, you say to Patrick, "You're welcome to join us as an observer. The retrospective starts at two o'clock."

Patrick replies, "We really appreciate your help. Happily Ever After is our flagship product, and the last thing we want to do is outsource our crown jewel. Unless we have to."

As you get up to leave, Patrick shakes your hand.

Before you know it, you're standing in the corridor faced with a challenging day ahead.

Continue with the adventure on page 251.

# Postpone Making Important Decisions

You don't have enough information right now to know whether or not Patrick's request to attend the retrospective is a good idea or a bad idea.

"I'd prefer to talk it through with the team first," you say. You've learned from experience that rushing to make a decision when you don't have to can cause serious problems later on.

"In any case, I'd be interested in seeing the output," says Patrick, "with the team's permission of course."

"I'll be sure to ask the team about that too," you say. "I'll let you know by email later today."

You know that if the team members agree, you could ensure confidentiality by typing up the information gathered in case people are worried that their comments can be traced back to them by their handwriting. There are many ways to share information effectively and safely. You can decide if this is necessary later on. There's no need to decide now.

Continue with the adventure on page 253.

## Review Your Mission

Before returning to the team space, you take time out to remind yourself of the goals of the engagement. It's important to always have the end in mind if you're to achieve your goals.

During your first meeting with Patrick, you cowrote the goals along with the acceptance criteria in the form of a user story. Below is what you both agreed on up front. Patrick made it clear back then that, given the recent poor delivery record of the team, delivery is now top priority, followed by ideas for helping the team improve its process.

PROVIDE RECOMMENDATIONS

As a management team, we need a list of recommendations so that the Dream Team delivers some value for this release and knows how to improve its team performance over time.

ACCEPTANCE CRITERIA

- Two or more delivery options outlined, each of which provide at least 50 percent of the original business case for the release

- Two or more recommendations for improving team performance

- Measures for gauging improvement in team performance

During that conversation, Patrick had reassured you that the project backlog contains items of significant business value. When you had asked about how the business value has been calculated and tracked to date, Patrick had explained that it's been difficult for the business to quantify the estimated value of the business proposition. He'd like to hear your ideas on how to do this at some point.

Continue with the adventure on page 35.

## Look Ahead

You take a moment to verify your progress in relation to your plan for the rest of the week. Since yesterday, you've been assessing the team's current performance through informal discussions with team members. This afternoon's project retrospective should provide more information on the challenges and obstacles that the team faces.

On Wednesday morning, you plan to baseline the project's current state. On Wednesday afternoon, you'll facilitate a planning session between the team and the product owner to come up with a short list of delivery options.

This potentially leaves you Thursday and Friday morning to do your recommendations report. Since the report will take between half a day to a day to prepare, there's some slack built into your schedule. You suspect you'll need it.

It's time to get Day 2 started with the team.

Continue with the adventure on page 39.

## Uninvited Guest

You ask everyone to gather around for a quick update on today's planned activities. To test the waters, you mention there's a possibility Patrick will be present at the project retrospective.

"I don't think that's a good idea," says Nancy.

"I thought you were here to help us," says Roger quietly.

"What doesn't make it a good idea?" you ask.

Matt, the former Scrum master, looks around the room and then says, "The management fixes the deadline and the budget but then allows the business to keep increasing the scope. At the rate we're going, we'll never finish the project."

Given the team's response, you decide to ask Patrick not to attend the meeting. You remind everyone to reconvene in the afternoon for the project retrospective and thank them for their time.

Continue with the adventure on page 37.

# Respect for People

Your gut feeling was right all along. What the team needs right now is the time and the space to share concerns in a safe, closed environment. Lesson relearned: listen to your gut.

You would have preferred to speak to Patrick face-to-face, but he's in a meeting for the rest of the day. Fortunately, you and Patrick have agreed on a communication protocol. You're welcome to see him in his office, but he may not always be in. For urgent matters, you can reach him on his cell phone. For less urgent matters, such as information sharing and notifications, you'll use email.

You email Patrick to let him know you've changed your mind. To get the most value out of the project retrospective, you advise that it's best to limit the attendance to team members only. You also mention that the team will decide at the end of the meeting whether or not the group feels comfortable sharing the output. You close by thanking him for his understanding and support.

Continue with the adventure on page 39.

# Team Privacy

You would have preferred to speak to Patrick face to face, but he's in a meeting for the rest of the day. Fortunately, you and Patrick have agreed on a communication protocol. You're welcome to see him in his office, but he may not always be in. For urgent matters, you can reach him on his cell phone. For less urgent matters, such as information sharing and notifications, you'll use email.

You email Patrick immediately to let him know that to get the most value out of the project retrospective, it's best to limit the attendance to team members. You also mention that the team will decide at the end of the meeting whether or not the group feels comfortable sharing the output. You close by thanking him for his understanding and support.

You were right to consult the team about Patrick's attendance. Acting respectfully toward everyone involved has enabled you to resolve even the toughest of problems in the past.

Continue with the adventure on page 39.

## Time to Reflect

Before you know it, it's time for the project retrospective. Everyone's arrived by the time you appear, everyone except Jason, that is.

"Glad to see you're here already!" you say with a smile. "We're scheduled to start in five minutes, so there's time to get a drink before we start."

"We won't make it to the bar and be back in time," says Matt. Ash sniggers, while Ben looks dead serious.

Jason arrives on time but remains standing by the door. You invite him to take a seat.

Continue with the adventure on page 40.

# Standoff

"This meeting is pointless," says Jason, with his arms crossed. "We all know exactly what we need to do, so why don't we just get on with it? What's this obsession with meeting after meeting? Talking instead of doing? I thought we were done with this 'fragile agile' nonsense."

This is the first time Jason has made a public complaint since you joined the team. It's unlikely to be the last. You can see Jason's body shaking as he tries to remain calm. He's also busy fidgeting with his left ear.

You now have a choice to make. Do you postpone the meeting until you've had a chance to clarify Jason's concerns and attitude with him one-on-one? This could push back coming up with an action plan indefinitely. What's more, the longer you wait, the harder it is to keep everyone together and moving in the right direction.

Or you could continue the meeting because it seems that the majority of the group wants to be there. As a change agent, you believe that everyone adds value and that there's a place for them on what Jim Collins calls the "bus of change." But that's only one-half of the equation. The other half requires an individual to be willing to get on the bus and come along for the ride.

Do you:

- find out what the team wants to do on page 41, or
- postpone the meeting on page 61?

# The Count

"If we are to be a real team," you say, looking each team member in the eye, including Jason, "we have to stick together. Let's take a team vote on what we'll do next. There are two options. Option 1 is to postpone this meeting. Option 2 is to carry on and do what we've gathered here to do: share our thoughts openly and honestly about where the project is at and how we want to move it forward together."

You explain how the voting will work. Everyone holds up a fist when they've decided on their option. When everyone's ready to vote, on a count of three, everyone shows a number of fingers to indicate his or her preferred option.

Jason remains by the door. Ash looks at Roger. Roger looks at Matt. Matt smiles back. Rebecca and Nancy smile too. Ben looks uncertain. One by one, fists go up in the air. The other two developers, Ethan and William, raise their fists too. The team is now waiting for Jason to vote.

"I won't vote, as I'm the facilitator," you say. "We wait until everyone's ready to vote. Take your time," you add.

Jason looks around the room and slowly raises his fist.

On the count of three, you ask everyone to show their fingers. "Let's go around the room. One by one, call out your vote loud and clear," you say.

Everyone votes to continue with the meeting, leaving Jason the odd one out. Never has the yawning divide between Jason and the rest of the team been so plain for all to see.

The moment passes and you ask Jason, in front of everyone, if he would be OK for the meeting to go ahead. To everyone's surprise, Jason nods and then takes a seat next to Matt.

Continue with the adventure on page 237.

# Agile Scrabble

"Let's go through the session plan," you say. "We'll use a kanban board to visualize the work we have planned for this project retrospective."

"We don't use Kanban here," says Jason. "We use Scrum."

You take this opportunity to clarify a common misunderstanding of the word *kanban*.

"The word 'kanban' has many different meanings, depending on the context," you explain. "In Japanese, *kanban* means "signal board." In the context of this meeting, I'm referring to a 'kanban board,' a tool for visualizing and tracking the activities we'll be covering in this session. I find that it helps everyone stay focused and get things done."

"Isn't kanban related to lean manufacturing?" asks Roger.

"Yes," you reply. "In the context of lean, kanban refers to a scheduling system for managing workflow that is also known as a 'kanban system.' It was developed by Taiichi Ohno at Toyota in order to improve and maintain a high level of production."

"My car's a Toyota," says William.

"In the context of software development, 'Kanban,' with an uppercase *K*, usually refers to applying a kanban system to an existing software development life cycle process. Key principles of such a system include visualizing work and limiting work in progress. We create a pull system by applying these principles, which means a team only pulls work in when it has spare capacity. Pull systems prevent teams from being overloaded."

"Pulling work sounds like a sensible idea," says Matt. "We're used to having work pushed onto us. Push systems result in overloaded teams."

"What's more, being an overloaded team makes life a total nightmare, for us at work and for those we love at home!" replies Rebecca, while everyone around the room nods.

"Can you give us some examples of how Kanban could work for us?" asks Jason.

Do you choose to:

- give a couple of examples of how Kanban can be applied on page 44, or
- continue with the exercise on page 47?

# Kanban Applied

It's your job to answer such questions from the team.

"Kanban is useful in many situations. I've seen Kanban used by production services teams and also by teams who want to improve an existing development process," you say.

You continue. "In the case of production services, it's hard to predict the amount of incoming issues and defects. Because Kanban allows you to plan on demand and establish a cadence that suits your type of work, you can focus on getting the work-in-progress items done and reprioritize the remaining To Do items as and when the issues and defects come in. This is unlike Scrum, which defines a specific cadence of one to four weeks and tells you when and how to do planning."

"It would be great to get rid of the defects," muses Nancy.

You nod and then continue. "Another effective use of Kanban is to improve existing processes," you say. "Since the flow of knowledge work is invisible, by visualizing your existing processes with Kanban, you can discover ways to improve it over time."

"I'm sure Patrick would be interested in hearing more about this use of Kanban," says Ben.

"If you want to find out more about how to achieve incremental and evolutionary process improvement, I suggest looking not just at kanban systems, but also at the Kanban method by David J. Anderson. It expands on the original concept to include applying kanban systems to creative knowledge work workflows or services," you say. "Also, some of you may be interested in Personal Kanban from Jim Benson and Tonianne DeMaria Barry. Jim and Tonianne show you how to organize your personal life using a kanban system."

"I'll have to try out a kanban board at home! My five year old loves structure and colorful stickies," says Rebecca.

"Maybe that will motivate her to make her bed and eat her vegetables!"

"We can explore these topics over lunch sometime if you like," you say.

"Maybe it's time we ran brown-bag sessions again," says Matt. "I'm sure Aidan from Team Predator would be pleased to help."

Continue with the adventure on page 46.

## No Silver Bullet

"In agile, there are lots of different methods. Scrum, Kanban, XP, DSDM... and the list goes on. So which agile method is better?" asks William.

"That depends on a number of factors, including the context and the nature of the work," you say. "There isn't an agile method that's 'one size fits all.'"

"That's reassuring," says Ben, "because I've been waiting for a silver bullet methodology for years and have been disappointed time after time."

"In any case, for a silver bullet to be useful, we first need to find ourselves a werewolf," says William, making people laugh and relax.

It's time to continue going through the session backlog.

Continue with the adventure on page 47.

## Agenda

"Let's continue with our project retrospective for now," you say.

You construct the session kanban board with three column headings: To Do, In Progress, and Done. Then you go through the items to be covered in the meeting, sticking one item at a time under the To Do column for everyone to see.

"We'll begin by setting the scene, and then we'll collect the data," you say. "After that, we'll sort through the data and finish by identifying improvement actions. We'll postpone the decision on which actions to take until tomorrow. We're on target to finish at four o'clock as planned. We'll take breaks as needed; just let me know when."

You move the "Scene Setting" sticky note into the In Progress column. You thank everyone for being present and restate the meeting objective: to exchange views on where the project is and how the team wants to move it forward.

"Who's going to see the output from our session?" Ben asks.

You explain that you'll ask for everyone's permission to share the content, with no names attached, with the managers and the product owner at the end of the session. There's no need to decide now. The team can wait until the end of the session.

Then you ask, "Do we all agree that Scene Setting is done?"

Matt and William nod, as do Nancy and Rebecca. "It's important we all agree an item is done before ticking it off," you add. Everyone nods, so you give the sticky note a big green tick and move it into the Done column.

Things seem to have calmed down. You use the kanban board to pace the rest of the meeting and keep everyone focused on the task at hand.

Continue with the adventure on page 48.

## Think Negative

The first exercise is to collect data. "We want to know, what sucks about this project?" you ask out loud.

Rebecca lets out a gasp, while Matt chuckles. "Where do I start?" he replies.

You hand out packs of red sticky notes, asking everyone to write down one answer per sticky note. Using red sticky notes is an easy and explicit way of distinguishing problems from tasks.

"Retrospective best practice says that we should always start with positive comments," interjects Roger.

You smile and suggest that everyone make this an exception. "You've got two minutes. Ready, steady, go!" You ding the bell, and the race toward continuous improvement begins.

The reason you've chosen to begin by brainstorming negatives about the project is because the negatives are clearly at the forefront of most people's minds. Externalizing the negatives early on in the process frees up people's minds to think creatively about the future.

Continue with the adventure on page 49.

## True Lies

After some rapid brainstorming, everyone, including Jason, has a pile of sticky notes with scribbles in front of them. Next, everyone takes a turn coming to the front of the room to read out his or her sticky notes and then stick them up, one by one. Duplicate sticky notes get stacked together as they appear.

After twenty intense minutes, the team takes a step back. For once, everyone is silent as the team contemplates the red collage and what it represents.

"This project really sucks," says Ben quietly.

"It's what I've been saying all along!" says Roger with a sigh of relief. During his one-on-one with you, Roger had mentioned his frustration at being part of a failing project. Now that that frustration is clearly visible and shared by others, the team can choose to do something about it. Or not.

"Most important of all, those red pieces of paper combine to tell our team's story," says Nancy. It seems Nancy's nostalgia has the last word on this occasion.

Continue with the adventure on page 50.

# Think Smart

It's time to move on to the fun bit. You ask people to form pairs, ideally with someone they don't know very well.

"That's stupid," says Jason, "we've been working together for over a year—for some of us, almost a decade."

"Never mind. I want to get to know you better," says Rebecca. You recall Rebecca had mentioned that she'd known Jason for some years now, and it seems that she and Jason are already good friends.

You continue. "Your mission as a whole team is to ensure there's at least one improvement action for each problem or complaint," you say. "In pairs, select someone else's problems to solve. Pick any problem, so long as it's not your pair's. Then write down one improvement action per green sticky note," you say while handing out packs of green. "Put the green sticky note next to its corresponding red sticky note when you're done."

You give the team fifteen minutes. To pace the exercise, you will ding the bell every five minutes.

"What if a problem's not solvable? There are plenty of those," says Jason.

"Come with me. My son says I eat impossible for breakfast!" says Rebecca as she takes Jason by the arm.

"Ready, steady, go!" you say. Ding! goes the bell.

"That must be the sound of continuous improvement," says Matt to William with a chuckle.

Continue with the adventure on page 51.

## Time Out

The bell rings. Time's up for identifying improvement actions. For each problem sticky note, there's now at least one corresponding green improvement sticky note on the board. And there are a few more smiles around the room.

You suggest a ten-minute break. The group disperses. Most people head over to the water cooler and coffee machine. Matt stays behind.

"You're doing a good job," he says. Matt tells you that the team's tried doing retrospectives themselves, and even got people from other teams to help facilitate. Yet no matter how hard they tried, the improvement actions never got done. That's why they stopped doing them altogether.

You nod and then say, "Thanks for the feedback and information, Matt. Meanwhile, I need a break!"

Do you:

- get yourself a coffee from the break room on page 52, or
- head over to the water cooler, and then return to tidy up the room on page 53?

## Sustainable Pace

There's always time for a break. Working at a sustainable pace has saved you more than once. It's all too easy to get caught up in an ever-growing mountain of work. Working harder and longer usually creates more problems than it solves, resulting in you spending more time fixing those problems instead of moving things forward.

What's more, as a facilitator and coach, you know you need to stay rested in order to keep calm and be effective.

On your way back to the meeting room, you bump into Patrick.

"It seems most of the team is happy with the way you're running the retrospective," says Patrick. "I haven't seen them talk so passionately about the project for a long time. Ben's concerned nothing will change, just like all the times we've tried before. I look forward to you proving both of us wrong."

Continue with the adventure on page 53.

## Treasure Map

People begin to return from their break. Ash, Roger, and Rebecca are exchanging ideas on how they can reduce the number of defects.

"Who's going to make all the improvements happen?" says Jason, wedged firmly in his seat, arms crossed.

"That depends," you reply. "We don't have to decide yet."

To complete sorting through the sticky notes, you co-create a process map with the team. You ask the team to describe the different steps a requirement goes through from idea conception to reaching the end user.

You write down each step on an index card as the team describes the process, and you stick them up in a horizontal row to visualize the current process. You then add arrows to link the steps together. Here are the process steps:

1. Requirements gathering
2. Production of test scripts
3. Design and architecture
4. Development
5. Dev testing
6. Sys testing
7. User acceptance testing
8. Release preparation
9. Release sign-off
10. Release

Then you ask the team to sort the problem-improvement clusters by problem according to the corresponding process step. This will show everyone where the problem hotspots are and how improvements can impact the existing process. The team has ten minutes.

Ding! goes the bell.

Continue with the adventure on page 54.

# Visible Impact

The team steps back to take a good look at the latest incarnation of their collage. It's so quiet you can hear a pin drop.

You ask the team to describe what they see.

Jason is the first to speak. "It hasn't reduced the number of things we need to fix."

"Jason's right. But arranging the sticky notes by the process steps helps us to more clearly see the dependencies and the impact of the improvement actions on the process itself," says Roger.

"It's also a better-looking piece of modern art now that it has a splash of green on it," says William. His comment reminds you of your conversation about his favorite hobby, painting with acrylics and using recycled materials.

Then there is an unexpected pause as Matt shuffles his feet. He coughs and then says, "It's the first time we've all worked as a team for a long time."

Continue with the adventure on page 55.

## Double Check

It's 3:50. Time to wrap up the session.

You hold up the sticky note labeled "Identify improvement actions." Everyone nods and shouts, "Done!"—everyone except Jason.

Matt gives Jason a nudge. Jason nods slowly, with arms still crossed.

You give the sticky note a big green tick and move it into the Done column.

It's been a long day. There's time to take a quick temperature reading of team morale and gather feedback on how the retrospective has gone.

Do you:

- hold a short meeting retrospective on page 56, or
- call it a day on page 59?

## Retrospect

"Before we end this session, let's take a vote on how the retrospective has gone using estimation poker," you say.

Instead of using fingers on only one hand, this time you ask everyone to vote out of ten using both hands. As they say, variety is the spice of life. Also, the larger range gives people a chance to be more expressive with the number they choose.

You explain that a ten means "That was excellent and worthwhile; I'm glad I participated." And a zero means "That was an utter waste of time. I'm a celebrity; get me out of here!"

Everyone holds up both fists when they're ready to vote.

On the count of three, you ask everyone to show their fingers. "Let's go around the room. One by one, call out your vote loud and clear," you say.

Continue with the adventure on page 57.

# Through the Looking Glass

Votes range from a high of 10 to a low of 5.

You ask the people who voted lowest for feedback first, and then ask those who voted the highest.

"Don't get me wrong," says Roger. "I found the session useful in terms of identifying what sucks and the improvement actions. I gave the session a 5 because I want to see the outcome of those actions first before deciding how useful the session was."

"But that's outside the scope of this session," says Ash. "I thought the session was excellent. It gave me the courage to finally speak up." Ash rated the session a 9.

"I gave the session a 10 because it felt like a breath of fresh air," says Matt. "It reminds me of what we're capable of when we work as a team. Also, the session goals were met and all the tasks got done!"

You tell everyone it's now "all play." Everyone's welcome, one at a time, to share the thinking behind their rating. You introduce the "talking token," a soft ball the size of your hand, which makes it easy to throw and, most important of all, easy to catch. Whoever has the talking token has the floor.

William requests the ball by raising his hand. William agrees with Roger's reasoning, but nonetheless he gave the session a 7 because it was the best-run retrospective he's attended because everyone participated. "In my opinion, getting people together to agree on the problems is the hard part. Implementing solutions should be easier. After all, that's what we're paid to do," he adds.

William throws the ball to Rebecca. She gave the session an 8. "Thanks to Jim for being a great facilitator. We can be a difficult bunch sometimes." Rebecca smiles. "Going through the retrospective has made me realize how much we can improve. Better still, how much of it is actually within our scope of control."

Rebecca throws the ball to Nancy. "I gave it a 9 because it was valuable and fun. I agree with Jason that we've got a lot of improving to do. The good news is that things that seemed impossible this morning now have tangible improvement actions. I'll be the first to admit that it's going to require hard work."

Jason signals for the ball. "I gave the session a 6 because it turned out to be better than expected. Thanks, Jim."

Jason throws the ball to Ben. "It was great to have the whole team together. That's mainly why I rated the session a 7. However, we've done activities like this one before and nothing has changed. I want to know what's going to be different this time around," says Ben.

"That depends on all of us," you reply.

Continue with the adventure on page 59.

## Made Public

You thank everyone for their input, enthusiasm, and feedback. You have one last question of the day to ask the team.

"Do I have the team's permission to share the content anonymously with the managers and the product owner?" you ask.

"In the spirit of collaboration and continuous improvement, I think we should share it," says Matt, taking the lead. "Let's vote on it. If you think we should share the information, raise your hand."

For the first time, almost everyone's hand goes up at the same time.

Continue with the adventure on page 60.

# Coach's Log: Day 2

February 2

ACTIVITIES

- First daily catch-up with Patrick
- Prep for project retrospective
- Project retrospective

WHAT WENT WELL

- Handled the first challenge—confrontation from Jason in front of the team—respectfully
- Consulted the team to determine if it was worth continuing with the meeting
- Identified the team has become ineffective in the norming stage of the Tuckman model—the retrospective marks the start of a return to the storming stage so that the team can improve.
- Got improvement actions for all our problems!

WHAT WENT WRONG

- Didn't spend enough time with Jason to better understand his concerns prior to the retrospective

PUZZLES

- How long will everyone stay on the bus of change?

IMPROVEMENT ACTIONS

- Spend more time individually with the quieter team members (such as William and Ash) to ensure everyone has a chance to voice their thoughts/concerns.
- Spend more time with Jason.

DAY RATING: 8/10

Continue with the adventure on page 81.

## Escape

You decide to postpone the meeting. This is neither the time nor the place to resolve the ensuing conflict between Jason, the team, and yourself.

You tell the whole team, "Thanks for coming. We are postponing today's meeting to tomorrow."

Jason rushes out of the room. Ash and Roger look disappointed. Matt stays behind to speak to you. Everyone else gets up to go.

Continue with the adventure on page 62.

# Outburst

With everyone gone except Matt, there is a moment of awkward silence.

Suddenly, you hear a loud thud outside the meeting room like fists hitting against the wall, followed by muffled shouting.

You recognize Jason's voice. It sounds like he's letting off some steam after what's just happened.

"Who the hell does that Jim think he is, waltzing into our team and telling us what to do. We've managed just fine without him to date and we certainly don't need him now," says Jason.

"What's an agile coach anyway? Most of the ones I've met have never been developers, so what value can they possibly bring to software development teams?" he continues.

"I know that Jim used to be a developer, so he should be the first to understand that developers don't need process. Tell us what your requirement is and we'll make it happen. Experts like me and Matt don't need process. Why is Matt still in there with him anyway?" asks Jason.

"I'll tell you what our top two problems are. There's Cassandra, who can't decide what she wants. The same goes for the rest of the product development team. They're just a waste of time. Then there's the junior developers like Roger, who should concentrate on translating the business rules into code instead of going on and on about the importance of teamwork. Except for me and Matt, we've got inexperienced developers with no idea what beautiful architecture looks like. They're too naive to appreciate the sophisticated framework we've created," says Jason, hoarse from all the shouting.

"I'm sick and tired of dealing with these people. I can't believe we're risking the future of our business with a bunch of amateurs," says Jason.

Jason's harsh words echo down the corridor as his footsteps fade away into the distance.

Continue with the adventure on page 64.

## Old Friends

Matt tells you about how he and Jason were the first developers to work on Happily Ever After. Back then, it didn't even have a name, just an idea that if the company offered the first online dating service, it could improve many people's lives. People would pay good money for that. Anything was worth a shot in the dot-com days.

Matt and Jason had gone to college together, and the company was a start-up funded by a bunch of professors. They had some of the smartest PhDs in the country leveraging the latest Web technology. It was a time when tech academics powered the IT revolution by a combination of sheer brilliance and stubbornness.

"As time went on, us techies became more and more set in our ways," says Matt with a grimace. "We became so certain that we were always right that there was no room left for opinion and input from others. As the codebase grew, so did our egos. And, with it, came keyman dependency."

Matt believes the confrontation between Jason and the team is the legacy of this past. The hero culture that developed over the years means that a handful of technologists are holding the company, and all the people in it, hostages. What kind of future can there be for such a company in crisis?

Matt is trying to be helpful by filling you in on the past, but after what's just happened with Jason, you need time to yourself to think.

Do you:

- go for a break on page 65, or
- continue chatting with Matt on page 79?

## Detour

You thank Matt and tell him you need a break. You suggest that you, Matt, and Ben meet up after lunch to explore options on how best to proceed.

Matt nods and heads back to the team space. You go for a walk and a coffee.

On your way back from the cafeteria, you take a detour to visit a team space covered in sticky notes with people sitting in pairs, working together in front of computers. It's time to make some new friends.

Continue with the adventure on page 66.

## Friend

You walk into the team space and talk to a guy standing by the kanban board.

You greet him with a smile and a firm handshake.

"Hi, I'm Jim," you say. "I've just joined the Dream Team as part of a continuous team improvement initiative."

"Nice to finally meet you, Jim. We've been waiting for you," says the stranger.

Continue with the adventure on page 67.

# Predator

It turns out you're talking to Rickard, Scrum master of Team Predator. Rickard is the Scrum master for the team's current sprint. They rotate the role around so that everyone in the team gets to have a go. What's more, the team takes collective responsibility for what a Scrum master does.

You discover that your presence in the company has caused quite a stir. Everyone's been talking about what you and the team are up to. Most important of all, the million dollar question remains the same, "Can you help the Dream Team and save the company?"

"Anything's possible if we work together," is your usual reply to such a question.

Over the years, the diversity of roles and responsibilities you've had has meant you've learned to play many parts, including that of Socrates, Sherlock Holmes, and the A-Team. And you've seen how working together can make the seemingly impossible possible.

The rest of the team now comes over, and people introduce themselves one at a time. The team makes you feel welcome.

"Best of luck," says Aidan, a developer, as he slaps you on the back. "You've got a tough nut to crack for sure!"

Everyone chuckles except you.

Continue with the adventure on page 68.

## Simple, Not Easy

Team Predator tells you they're the second team to have adopted agile at Love Inc. Everything they've learned about agile has initially been from the Dream Team: the good, the bad, and the ugly. Eventually, Team Predator and the Dream Team went their separate ways because they disagreed about the fundamentals of agile. Unlike the Dream Team, Team Predator preferred to stick to the basics and get them right before deviating from standard agile practices.

"At first we couldn't believe how difficult something so seemingly simple like the daily scrum could be," explains Annabel, a business analyst. "To start with, we just assumed it was a meeting for management, which made it a drag. Then someone suggested that we apply the Scrum principle of 'inspect and adapt,' and that's what we did."

Seth, a developer, smiles at Annabel and continues telling the team's story. "After the first few daily scrums, we would hold a ten-minute retrospective after each one to figure out what worked well and what didn't. Then we would make the necessary improvements and inspect and adapt some more, until we eventually figured out that the daily scrum was really a chance for team members to sort themselves out. Through lots of experimentation, we learned to make it work for us."

Continue with the adventure on page 69.

## True Agile

Team Predator are adamant that they're no experts when it comes to agile. Instead of "doing agile" or "being agile," the team refers to what they do as "learning agile."

"Agile's a journey that never ends," says Aidan, "at least according to those who don't just talk the talk but walk the walk." He strikes his chest with his fist as he says this to show his sincerity.

Everyone laughs, including you.

"We're in it for the long run!" says Barry, a tester wearing a T-shirt that says "I don't have to be superhero to do great things." "Even though we call our two-week time boxes sprints, it's more like running a marathon. That's why we try to work at a sustainable pace."

"It can be tough at times, though," says Rickard, "so we remind each other by saying, 'Show me the money!' We're referring to the business value of the requirements, of course, to ensure we don't waste unnecessary time on low value and costly items that aren't really needed."

"Absolutely!" says François, their product owner from Dijon. François tells you how he went from sitting on the third floor full-time to sitting with the team on the first floor for two days a week shortly after the project began. He describes learning agile as requiring serious dedication. "It's also good for the heart," he says as he gives Annabel a wink.

The walk has done you good. You're glad to have discovered such friendly neighbors. You feel recharged and are ready for the challenge ahead. You thank everybody on Team Predator for their time and their stories.

As Rickard walks you out, he tells you, "We're always learning how to apply agile better. Maybe we can meet up sometime to exchange ideas?"

You say that if everything goes well this week, your contract may be extended and you two can catch up next week when you'll have more time.

As you leave, Aidan calls out, "Come back and visit us whenever you need to!"

You turn to wave and smile.

Continue with the adventure on page 71.

# Ego

After your break, you arrive to find Ben and Matt whispering in a huddle.

"We have to act fast," Matt says. He tells you Jason will do whatever it takes to derail the project just to prove how smart he is in comparison with the rest of the developers. "Jason and I have worked together for a long time. I have great respect for his technical expertise, but it's vital we remove toxic keyman dependencies if we want our project and company to succeed."

Ben has grown quiet. You ask Ben to share his thoughts.

As Scrum master, Ben wants to create an environment where everyone can flourish. "I want to believe that we can succeed together as a team," he says. "It's easy for us to break up the team now, but it's not the only option. Maybe we need to talk things through with Jason and see if he'd be willing to work together."

You thank them both for being open and candid. You explore a few options with Matt and Ben regarding how best to regain momentum on your engagement.

One option is for you to confront Jason directly about this morning's incident and together figure out a way for him and the team to proceed together.

A second option is for you to escalate the problem to Patrick and ask him for advice and help.

A third option is to arrange a three-person conversation between Patrick, Jason, and yourself to figure out how best to help the team move forward.

Do you:

- confront Jason on your own on page 72,
- consult Patrick and ask him for help on page 78, or
- arrange a three-person conversation on page 76?

## Apologies

You bump into Jason in the break room. He looks away.

"Can we have a talk?" you ask. Jason nods.

The break room is empty, so you grab a table.

"I'm sorry about what happened at the project retrospective this afternoon," you say. "I should have prepared better for the project retrospective by spending more time with you to understand the current situation. What's more, I couldn't care less if we used agile or some other methodology," you add. "My priority is to help the team build the best product they can."

For the first time, Jason looks surprised. He remains silent while fidgeting with his left ear.

Continue with the adventure on page 73.

# Old School

Eventually Jason speaks up. "None of the concepts in agile are new," he says. "Most of them exist in older methodologies that you're too young to remember."

"That's true," you reply. "Agile combines many ideas from lean and effective management. I consider agile as a second chance to apply these values, principles, and practices to help us improve the way we work."

Although Jason understands how agile could work in principle, he tells you this organization is different. "We're the exception to the rule. It won't work here."

You've heard this response many times before.

Jason continues. "To be honest, I'm skeptical about agile. We've been doing it for ages, and all I can see are problems emerging one after another."

To explain why the problems keep surfacing, you compare the organization with a riverbed. "Agile works by lowering the water level to reveal all the 'rocks,' or blockers, that exist in an organization's processes and culture," you say. "It's up to people to decide what to do about those rocks."

You continue. "Processes don't fail. People do. That's because if processes don't work, we can change them."

Jason uncrosses his arms for the first time. You take this chance to explain your view of agile.

You say that it's taken you many attempts to appreciate that agile is a tool and, like any tool, its effectiveness is context-dependent. With experience, you've also come to realize that it's so much more than a tool. It's a mindset shift. Apply its values and principles consistently, and agile can be a catalyst for creating a culture of continuous improvement, resulting in enduring change.

"That's a lofty ambition," says Jason as he crosses his arms once again.

It's time you get to the point. "There are going to have to be some changes if we're to get the team through this," you say. "The team needs your help to succeed."

There is a long silence. Jason stands up. Your conversation with Jason is over.

Continue with the adventure on page 75.

## Coach's Log: Day 2

February 2

ACTIVITIES

- First daily catch-up with Patrick
- Prep for project retrospective
- Postponed project retrospective
- Met Team Predator
- Met with Ben and Matt to discuss the Jason situation
- Met with Jason

WHAT WENT WELL

- Handled the first challenge—confrontation from Jason in front of the team—respectfully
- Team Predator friendly and supportive of my engagement

WHAT WENT WRONG

- Didn't spend enough time with Jason to better understand his concerns prior to the retrospective

PUZZLES

- How long until we have a list of improvement actions?
- How to create understanding between Jason and me?
- Will Jason stay with the team or choose to go?

IMPROVEMENT ACTIONS

- Spend more time individually with the quieter team members (including Jason) to ensure everyone has a chance to voice their thoughts/concerns.

DAY RATING: 5/10

Continue with the adventure on page 146.

## Missing in Action

Patrick is out meeting a client this afternoon, and Jason has disappeared. No one knows where Jason has gone.

You decide to email a meeting invite to Patrick, Jason, and yourself for tomorrow morning. You schedule the meeting immediately after your daily catch-up with Patrick so that you can fill him in on what's happened beforehand.

Continue with the adventure on page 77.

# Coach's Log: Day 2

February 2

ACTIVITIES

- First daily catch-up with Patrick
- Prep for project retrospective
- Postponed project retrospective
- Met Team Predator
- Met with Ben and Matt to decide on options for handling the Jason situation

WHAT WENT WELL

- Handled the first challenge—confrontation from Jason in front of the team—respectfully
- Members of Team Predator friendly and supportive of my engagement

WHAT WENT WRONG

- Didn't spend enough time with Jason to better understand his concerns prior to the retrospective

PUZZLES

- How long until we have a list of improvement actions?
- Will Jason stay with the team or go?

IMPROVEMENT ACTIONS

- Spend more time individually with the quieter team members (such as William and Ash) to ensure everyone has a chance to voice their thoughts/concerns.
- Also spend more time with Jason.

DAY RATING: 6/10

Continue with the adventure on page 140.

# Sound the Alarm

You walk over to Patrick's office. You hadn't expected to need to escalate so early on. Still, if there's one thing you've learned over the years, it's "Ask for help." You've also learned that if you're not sure you need help, ask anyway. More often than not, you need it.

You continue to think about the situation with Jason. You catch yourself sighing and say out loud, "Everyone adds value." It's the best way to hear an important reminder after a long day.

When you get to Patrick's office, you find he's out meeting a client this afternoon. It looks like you have a second chance to resolve the blocker yourself.

Continue with the adventure on page 72.

# Team Predator

You invite Matt for a walk and a coffee.

On your way back from the cafeteria, Matt points out a nearby team space that is covered in sticky notes, with people sitting in pairs, working together in front of computers.

"That's Team Predator," Matt says. It turns out Team Predator was the second team in the company to start using agile. They started six weeks after the Dream Team. At first, both teams supported one another, and then things got competitive.

The Dream Team didn't think agile worked "out of the box" given the company's unique situation, so they quickly adapted it to fit as best they could.

Team Predator chose to do the opposite and followed agile by the book, considering all deviation as cheating or giving in.

With hindsight, Matt now appreciates both teams' perspectives and believes there's a third option, a middle way between the two.

"We felt so much pressure as the first team to try agile that I now realize we were arrogant. We thought we knew better than what the textbooks told us," says Matt. "Looking back, I do recall reading about *shu-ha-ri*, a Japanese martial art concept on how to master a skill. It describes a three-step iterative process that begins with mimicking, followed by experimenting and finally innovating. I see now that the Dream Team leaped straight into innovating before we really understood the fundamentals."

Listening to Matt's reflections reminds of how far you yourself have yet to travel on that journey of continuous improvement.

You would have liked to have met Team Predator that afternoon. Now you're left wondering what a team with such a name eats for breakfast. That's a puzzle to solve for another day.

Meanwhile, it's time for more chocolate chip cookies. You tell Matt you'll meet him and Ben in the meeting room.

Continue with the adventure on page 71.

# Unexpected Encounter

It's Day 3, and you head over to Patrick's office as usual. The project retrospective can be considered a success. In spite of this, you notice a tight knot in your stomach. You take a deep breath in, then out.

As you enter Patrick's office, you notice he's not alone.

"Morning, Jim," says Patrick. "I'd like to introduce you to Cassandra, the Dream Team's product owner. I've been keeping Cassandra up-to-date on our progress."

Cassandra explains she cut short her business trip in order to offer her support for the changes ahead. She suggests the two of you meet later on this morning to talk things over. In particular, she's concerned about the poor communication between herself and the team, not to mention the high number of defects during user acceptance testing. You arrange to meet Cassandra in her office at eleven o'clock.

You give a quick update on what you did yesterday and suggest that you all go over to the team space to see the output of the project retrospective for yourselves.

While Cassandra declines because she's busy with meetings, Patrick accepts your invitation.

Continue with the adventure on page 82.

# Greed and Gluttony

On your way over to the team space, Patrick asks you how the team's situation compares to those of other teams with whom you've worked. You assure him that it isn't at all unusual.

"Every team follows a cycle, much like the four seasons," you say. "At present, the team's between autumn and winter. This means that they've been doing the same things the same way for a while and are now stuck in a rut. Yesterday, we made that rut visible, along with all the other problems we face."

Patrick tells you that the current situation is reminiscent of the extenuating circumstances that made the team try agile in the first place. The company was in dire straits at the time, which forced the team members, and the whole company, to rethink the way they built and delivered their software.

Back in the early days, enthused by the large amount of seed funding, the business came up with a deluge of ideas that simply kept growing. Many of the ideas were excellent, which meant that the business wanted to implement them all at once.

"Therein lies the way to madness," says Patrick, shaking his head at the memory of those days. He compares it with being ravenous at a buffet, attempting to eat everything in sight all at the same time. "Most people's brains would short-circuit before they could get indigestion. We blew a circuit and just kept gorging."

Continue with the adventure on page 83.

## Tip of the Iceberg

Patrick is concerned that those days are coming back. The Dream Team's underdelivery of product features in the past three months has provided a reason for the management team to rethink its software development strategy, with talk of near-shoring and far-shoring options as the company looks to move into the global market. What's more, the rapidly ballooning backlog is creating more and more pressure on an already underperforming team.

Patrick confides in you. "Many of the Dream Team members set out on the start-up journey with us. I think many of them still believe in the product, even though people like Jason may have lost sight of that. I'm prepared to make tough decisions when it comes to preserving what we've achieved so far."

Patrick continues. "What concerns me most is that changing the way IT works will not be enough. Transforming the way we work with the business is when the real challenge begins."

Continue with the adventure on page 84.

## Team View

When you reach the team space, Ben stands up to greet you both.

You ask Ben to walk Patrick through the process and output of yesterday's project retrospective. Ben glosses over the confrontation between you and Jason that nearly stopped the retrospective from happening at all.

He begins by presenting the top five problems according to the team. He is able to do this because after the retrospective, when everyone got back to the team space, Roger led a team-voting exercise to identify what everyone thought were the top five problems.

Continue with the adventure on page 85.

## Grave Problems

Ben explains Roger's approach for determining how many votes everyone got. "According to mathematical theory, to guarantee you get a prioritized list, you take the total number of items and then divide by three," he says.

Ben continues. "In the Dream Team's case, since 15 problems divided by 3 is 5, everyone got five votes to cast. If someone preferred a particular option above all the others, they could cast all their votes for that option."

You're familiar with this formula and find it effective. You smile because it's the first instance of self-organization by the Dream Team since your arrival.

Ben shows you and Patrick the list of improvement actions for the top five problems without going into too much detail about each sticky note. Ben understands that, as a senior manager, Patrick's only interested in seeing the big picture.

The Dream Team's top five problems are these:

1. The details of the requirements are unclear.

2. The product owner is not available to answer questions when needed.

3. The team consistently fails to deliver the stories that are planned for a sprint.

4. More time is spent on fixing defects than on implementing stories.

5. More time is spent on analyzing stories than on implementing them during a sprint.

Do you:

- hear what Patrick thinks about the problems on page 86, or
- get a different perspective on page 88?

## Chance

Patrick is a good listener, but he seems quieter than usual. After a long pause, he says, "Last night, I watched a webinar called 'Scaling Agile Adoption.' The presenter quoted many statistics. The one that struck me most is that, according to the presenter, only 26 percent of a development team's effort contributes to a project's success. The rest comes down to people and managerial approach."

Patrick continues. "The speaker said the problems with software projects have never been about technology; they've always been about people. Regardless of how accurate his statistics are, that's the same conclusion I've come to after my twenty years in software development."

"That's been my experience too," says Ben. He goes on to explain how this morning he sorted out the actions into two lists, side by side, one column for what the team could do on its own and another that requires the management's help.

"Of course I'll do this exercise again with the team, but I wanted to get an idea of what we could do right away to make things better," Ben says. He adds, "Jim's presence has helped bring the team together. Maybe not all of us, but the majority of us. We want to stay together and deliver the project."

Patrick takes a picture of the two lists of actions to take away with him. He then says to Ben, "You do your bit as a team, and we'll do our best to help as management. We all want to make this work."

Time's up with Patrick. He shakes hands and thanks you both for doing a good job.

Continue with the adventure on page 87.

## Desperate Remedies

When Patrick's gone, Ben says he's got something important to tell you.

"I overheard Patrick telling one of the managers last week that Love Inc. has a number of choices when it comes to the future of software development. They can choose to outsource IT entirely or address the challenges we have one by one, beginning with the Dream Team," Ben says.

According to Ben, management can either keep the team together as is or split the team up and redistribute the people across other teams. Or they could disband all existing teams and shuffle people around in the hope that a change in team members would be enough to reinvigorate everyone and give the organization a morale boost.

"Whichever choice they pick, it won't count for much unless they address the root cause of all the problems," says Ben.

"In my opinion, the rift between the business and IT has become a chasm. It may be too late to build a bridge to meet each other halfway," he continues.

"One more thing," says Ben. "Patrick said yesterday that he's prepared to wait until after hearing your recommendation before deciding what to do with the team. Whatever management decides to do next with the Dream Team will set a precedent for the entire IT department going forward," says Ben.

Continue with the adventure on page 88.

## Next Steps

Your gut tells you it's time to get another perspective on the situation before your meeting with Cassandra this morning. One way to do this is by meeting the second team to adopt agile at Love Inc. They call themselves Team Predator.

Before you go off, you ask Ben to get the team together to review the retrospective output, vote on the priorities of problems, and capture additional insights. You explain that it's always good to look at things after a good night's rest, especially for validating information and refining ideas.

Continue with the adventure on page 89.

# Predator

You walk into the team space and speak to a guy standing by the kanban board. You greet the stranger with a smile and a firm handshake.

"Hi, I'm Jim," you say. "I've just joined the Dream Team as part of a continuous team improvement initiative."

"Nice to finally meet you, Jim. We've been waiting for you," he replies.

It turns out you're talking to Rickard, the current Scrum master of Team Predator. In this team, everyone takes turns doing the role so that everyone gets to have a go.

You discover from Rickard that your presence in the company has caused quite a stir. Everyone's been talking about what you and the team are up to. Most important of all, the million-dollar question remains the same: Can you help the Dream Team and save the company?

To which you reply, "Yes, so long as everyone works together." As for how you would make this happen, you see yourself as part Socrates, part Sherlock Holmes, and part A-Team.

The rest of the team now comes over and introduces themselves one at a time. They make you feel welcome.

"Best of luck," says Aidan, an exceptionally tall and enthusiastic developer, as he slaps you on the back. "You've got a tough job ahead of you!"

Everyone chuckles except you.

Continue with the adventure on page 90.

## Humble Beginnings

You ask the team members to tell you about their agile experience.

They explain that they're the second team to have adopted agile at the company. Everything they've learned has been from the Dream Team: the good, the bad, and the ugly. Eventually, Team Predator took a different route because, unlike the Dream Team, they preferred to stick to the basics and get them right before deviating from the standard agile practices.

"For instance, we were all surprised at how hard something like the daily scrum could be," explains Annabel, a business analyst. "At first, we just assumed it was a meeting for management, which was a drag. Then someone suggested we apply the Scrum principle of "inspect and adapt," and that's what we did."

Seth, a developer, continues with the story. "After the first few daily scrums, we would hold a ten-minute retrospective to figure out what worked well each time and what didn't. Then we would make the necessary improvements and inspect and adapt some more. After a week, we figured out that the daily scrum was primarily for us to track our own progress. All this experimentation helped us improve!"

"That's the most important thing about learning agile," says Aidan. "It's hard work, but it's well worth it. What you get out really depends on how much you choose to put in."

Danny and Wendy, the other two developers, agree.

Continue with the adventure on page 91.

# Dog Eat Dog

You ask the team to tell you about the top challenges an agile team faces at Love Inc.

"It's hard to speak for all the teams," explains Aidan. "We used to be a close-knit, family-run kind of business. Then the business took off big time (Who would have thought there'd be so many mutually attractive singles out there until we came along?), and the family start-up went corporate."

Rickard explains that none of the agile teams share their experiences with one another because they're incentivized to compete with one another. "It's a bit strange, given that we're all developing the same product. None of the teams actively sabotage each other, but we're certainly not encouraged to help other teams!"

"The story gets messier when you start looking at how the business works," says Vanessa, a developer who seems tiny next to Aidan. Vanessa explains that product owners are pitted against one another for getting their ideas implemented, to the detriment of the company. "It's no wonder our codebase looks like Frankenstein's monster! It's a nightmare to code and test. All the teams know this."

Continue with the adventure on page 256.

## Overloaded

It's time for your meeting with Cassandra, the Dream Team's product owner.

"Given you're here to help, I'm going to tell you everything," says Cassandra. "There's so much going on at the moment, from getting the company ready to go public, to my maternity leave in three months."

"Congratulations," you say.

"For which piece of news?" asks Cassandra. "The teams don't know about going public, by the way. I suspect they're probably feeling the pressure, though."

Cassandra knows she's been neglecting the team when it comes to requirements, but she's doing the best she can. She's got a job and a half on top of being a product owner, and no one ever told her that being a product owner would take up so much of her time.

What's more, she's got at least half a dozen different business people with completely different views on where to take the product. It's like trying to manage a circus. "Or as you techies say, 'like herding cats,'" she adds.

Cassandra says she simply doesn't have any more time than the one hour per week she currently gives the Dream Team. And she knows it's not enough.

And then there's the team space. She simply can't bear walking into that place. Cassandra exclaims, "All those sticky notes stuck higgledy-piggledy on the wall. Nothing's lined up properly. It makes me feel physically sick to work in that place."

She continues. "Also, there's something so childish about agile. I find it downright patronizing. Why does everyone need to tell each other exactly what they're up to? We're adults. We should be able to organize ourselves without resorting to felt-tip pens and sticky notes!"

Do you:

- address Cassandra's concerns on page 94, or
- find out more about the company culture from Cassandra on page 96?

## Open Dialogue

You respect Cassandra's views of agile and thank her for the feedback on the team space. You know that Cassandra has a background in lean and six sigma, so you begin by emphasizing the link between those two approaches and agile to establish a common understanding between you and Cassandra.

"Agile has been heavily inspired by lean," you explain. "Agile, like lean, optimizes the value chain by eliminating waste. Agile also focuses on business value to ensure that whatever we do is of value to the end customer and the organization."

Cassandra stops fiddling on her Blackberry. "Go on," she says. "Now I'm intrigued."

You continue with your explanation. "As with learning anything new, the experience usually resembles a J-curve, with a notable dip in performance as people come to grips with a new way of working before performance increases with practice and experience over time."

You tell Cassandra that, for now, the team will make the most of the time she can spend with them. You'll be helping the team to better visualize its work so that everyone can see where they are in the project, how much is done, and how much work stands between the team and the finish line. This will help pinpoint where focus and effort are most needed.

"The kanban board is a way of helping the team manage its work and track progress, just like in lean," you say. "The sticky notes are a way of helping people break down large items into smaller, more manageable pieces of work. The sticky notes also help liven up what would otherwise be a monotone workspace."

You conclude by saying, "We'll tidy up the team space from now on. Maybe you can come over later on to test whether or not we've improved the team space enough for you to work comfortably with the team there?"

"Closing the feedback loop, I like that," says Cassandra with a nod.

A beep from her phone, and Cassandra's busy fiddling on her Blackberry again. She looks up just long enough to say, "Let me know when. I'll do my best to help."

Continue with the adventure on page 98.

## Selfish Programming

You ask Cassandra to describe the company culture in three words.

"That's simple!" she says. "Just between you and me, I'd say 'well-meaning,' 'misguided,' and 'eat-your-own.'" Cassandra rolls her eyes and then adds, "There are also plenty of other words for describing our culture."

You ask Cassandra to give examples of what she means by her choice of words.

She explains "well-meaning" in terms of the way in which the vision of Victoria Amore, the founder of Love Inc., continues to inspire people to work for the company. "Victoria believes everyone in the world has a right to find true love," says Cassandra. "I'm inclined to agree with her."

According to Cassandra, Love Inc.'s business model has been a key driver of its success. By playing the role of matchmaker, Love Inc. promises to help each client find a lifelong companion in five different dates or fewer. "We're so confident in our search algorithm and pool of candidates that our premium service comes with a find-love-or-your-money-back guarantee. It's one heck of a unique selling point!"

Cassandra moves on to her second descriptive word. By "misguided," she means that the business insists on throwing away everyone's hard work by pursuing low-value, high-cost, high-risk items instead of those with high return on investment.

Last, but not least, by "eat-your-own," she's referring to the way in which people are encouraged to compete against one another through a reward structure of pay, promotion, and bonuses that is biased toward personal gain.

"Make what you will of my six words," says Cassandra as she looks you straight in the eye. "And what about other people? What do they say?"

Do you:

- move on with the conversation on page 98, or
- share what Team Predator told you on page 99?

## Move On

"Maybe we can continue this conversation another time. I should go see how the team is doing," you say. You thank Cassandra for her time.

You mention you're interested in seeing more of the product roadmap in the near future because you have some techniques for identifying minimum scope, or what's also known as the "minimum viable product."

This information strikes a chord with Cassandra. "I'll try to drop by tomorrow, in case the team has any questions for me," says Cassandra. You shake hands and go your separate ways.

Continue with the adventure on page 100.

## Lost

You summarize what Team Predator told you in one word. "Competitive," you say while preserving your source's anonymity. You go on to elaborate that the people you've spoken to are concerned by the way in which they're pitted against one another for success.

"I don't think we'll ever become truly agile," says Cassandra. "Our organization is just not set up for it. It would take a serious culture change—and a return to the company's original values of care, consideration, and collaboration."

It's time you return to the team. You thank Cassandra for her time and you go your separate ways.

Continue with the adventure on page 100.

## Do Food

You pass by Team Predator on your way back from Cassandra's office and decide to make a quick stop.

"Didn't think you'd be back so soon!" says Aidan with a big smile. "How can we help?"

You invite the team to have lunch with the Dream Team at noon.

"Some of the others are busy with backlog refinement at the moment. I'll let them know," says Aidan.

"I'll swing by just before so we can all walk over together," you say. If only everything in this place was as straightforward as organizing lunch.

Continue with the adventure on page 101.

# Catch-Up

You return to the Dream Team to find that a few of the sticky notes from the project retrospective have been shuffled around. In addition, there are now two lists of prioritized actions from the team, one for the team and one for management.

"We've been busy!" Ben says with a smile. "By the way, our kanban board needs updating."

Matt walks over. "How was the meeting with Cassandra?"

"Let's have a quick huddle," you say loudly enough for everyone in the team to hear.

Continue with the adventure on page 102.

## The Gift of Feedback

You share the information you've gathered. You observe that Cassandra's overloaded, like most people in this organization. You suggest that everyone work together to find ways of making better use of her limited time.

"Meanwhile, Cassandra has some feedback regarding the team space," you say. You explain that she finds the kanban board difficult to make sense of.

Roger jumps up and says, "But it's for the team!"

You agree, then highlight how much more valuable it could be if others who wish to know the team's progress could see for themselves, especially when there's no one around to ask. "In well-functioning teams, a product owner is considered part of the team," you add.

You continue. "In my experience, a team's workspace can tell you a lot about the team. To paraphrase the Toyota way, 'Everything a team produces is a reflection of the effectiveness of its teamwork.'"

Ben says, "We can tidy up the kanban board and space today. Especially if it means Cassandra would be feel more comfortable working with us."

"Who knows? It might even make her feel like sitting with us," adds William.

You thank everyone for their time. You mention that you're having lunch with Team Predator and that everyone's invited.

At noon, the usual crowd and Team Predator walk over to the cafeteria together—everyone except Roger, who's preparing for his beach holiday, and Jason, who declines because of a prior lunch appointment.

Continue with the adventure on page 103.

# Food for Thought

"It's been ages since we've had lunch together," says Rickard to Ben, one Scrum master to another.

Rickard's enthusiasm is met with silence.

"As I recall, it must be almost six months ago. Wasn't it just before we had that big argument about the concept of *shu-ha-ri*?" pipes up François.

At this point, Matt coughs to clear his throat as much as to clear the air. "As the first team to go agile, I now realize how arrogant we've become. Since Jim's been here, we've been taking a good long look at what's been happening in the team."

This is followed by a longer silence, before Aidan says, "We've had a rough ride too." Turning to Seth, a fellow developer from Team Predator, he says, "Do you remember all the quarrels we had at the beginning about daily scrums?"

Seth describes how they'd get so frustrated with one another about not 'getting it,' which wasn't limited to daily scrums alone, that they'd literally take it out on each other on the soccer field every Wednesday night.

"Yeah, sorry again about the ankle, François," says Aidan, and everyone laughs. Aidan seems to be able to lighten up the mood in even the most awkward of situations.

Ben finally speaks up. He describes agile as a contact sport with oneself as much as with others. "It frustrates the hell out of me that I still don't get most of it, and there are days when I don't feel agile at all."

"Especially on Mondays for me!" says Aidan. Everyone laughs again.

It turns out the teams finish sprints on Fridays and start them on Mondays because of weekend releases. Aidan says, "A common problem we experience with starting on a Monday and finishing on a Friday is that at least one person from the team is usually away on one or both of those days. This makes sprint planning a lot harder."

"That's one of the key reasons it's best practice to start and finish a sprint on either a Tuesday, Wednesday, or Thursday," you say.

Continue with the adventure on page 105.

# Teams Reunited

You change the topic. "How often do all the agile teams get together?" It's your turn to make everyone laugh.

"Never," says Aidan.

"Not often enough," says Ash.

"What's this I hear about teams competing against each other?" you ask. Everyone now jumps in and says how wrong and messed up the incentives are. Your table is creating so much noise that everyone else in the cafeteria turns around to see what's happening.

You wave to them to indicate that everything is okay. You overhear someone say, "Never mind those guys: the agile teams are a noisy bunch. Just watch; they'll be getting out their sticky notes any minute now."

Meanwhile, Rickard and Ben have agreed to arrange a regular meetup between the teams so that they can exchange stories and experiences.

"Sounds like 'Agile Anonymous' to me," says Aidan. "Best we do it over some beers!" Everyone laughs and gets up to go back to work.

You notice Rickard and Ben shake hands before going their separate ways.

Continue with the adventure on page 106.

## Hope and Help

You catch up with Aidan as everyone heads back to their respective team space.

"Thanks for helping out the Dream Team," you say.

"No problem," says Aidan. "Thanks for arranging lunch. We appreciate you being around. It's a nice change to have someone who listens to what we have to say."

Then Aidan gives you a big grin. "To be honest, most of us had given up on the Dream Team," he says. "Jason wouldn't let us introduce the latest development tools, let alone agile technical practices. How do you have a conversation with someone who already knows everything there is to know?"

Aidan admits that most of the dev teams are still working in the Dark Ages, and not just the Dream Team. It wasn't until recently that Team Predator succeeded at having frequent check-ins throughout the day, nightly builds, and automated continuous integration for all their modules.

"We've been doing test-driven development for a while, but we are by no means experts. Regression testing is still manual and is the next biggest source of waste and risk we want to tackle," Aidan adds.

He describes their software product framework as a behemoth, and it's taken them a long time to decouple their modules from the core codebase in order to make their code more robust. Team Predator hopes to put Jez Humble and David Farley's book on continuous delivery to good use soon.

"Best get back to my team," says Aidan. "No rest for the wicked. Thanks again for your help."

Continue with the adventure on page 107.

## Rocks

Judging by the noise level and smiles in the Dream Team's team space, lunching with Team Predator has had a positive effect.

You ask everyone to gather by the kanban board.

The project retrospective output has surfaced what the team thinks the problems are. Now it's time to expose the extent of those problems for all to see.

"It's time to visualize all our work," you say. You explain that the exercise serves three purposes. First, it exposes the challenges faced by the team in its daily work, also known as "rocks" or "blockers." Second, it gives the team a chance to update the kanban board with the latest information. Third, it's an opportunity to improve the presentation of the board itself.

The exercise should result in ideas for increasing the flow of work through the team, as well as help Cassandra feel more comfortable in the team space so that she may be willing to spend more time with the team.

You begin by giving everyone five minutes to brainstorm all the work items they've completed and all the work items they're currently working on, as well as any work items they plan to start, one item per sticky note. Each item should take no more than half a day's work. Also, everyone's welcome to reuse stickies for work items that are already on the kanban board.

Ding! goes the bell.

Continue with the adventure on page 108.

## Art Attack

Next, you ask the team members to announce their work items.

People take turns going up to the board, reading out their sticky notes one at a time and then sticking them under the corresponding headings of To Do, In Progress, or Done.

"This feels more like an art lesson than work," says Rebecca.

"We're going to have to be creative to sort this out," says William as everyone watches the In Progress column become more and more cluttered with sticky notes.

You notice Jason fidgeting with his left ear when it becomes obvious that he has the most sticky notes to stick up.

"It's getting really messy fast!" says Ash as he wades through his pile of sticky notes.

"Art often gets messier before it becomes beautiful," you say with a smile. This makes Matt and Ben chuckle.

"Here's hoping!" says Matt with his fingers crossed.

All this activity lasts around forty-five minutes. You ding the bell to signal break time.

"How long do we need for a break?" you ask.

Roger suggests five minutes. Ben says it's never only five minutes. Matt smiles and shouts, "Sustainable pace!" Everyone agrees to ten.

Continue with the adventure on page 109.

## Quiet

You bring out a box of Twinkies.

"I thought they quit making those," says Rebecca when she comes back with a coffee.

"Lucky for us, they're being made again!" replies Ethan.

"I'm really enjoying this modern art stuff," says William with a wry smile. "I only wish it wasn't made out of all the work we have to do!"

Most of the team is now gathered at the board, munching on their Twinkies and staring in stunned silence at the humongous challenge before them.

Continue with the adventure on page 110.

# Bringing Out the Dead

"Now we're going to make this mess work for us," you say. "Everyone take a small step back. What do you see?"

"Lots of work in progress," says Roger.

"Notice its stark contrast to the Done column, which only has a single item," says William in the voice of an art critic.

Nancy sticks her hand up. "On second thought, I've just remembered I've got a query to clarify for that item, so it's not really done." Nancy struggles to find room for her sticky note in the In Progress column and ends up sticking it on top of others.

"At least it doesn't feel so lonely anymore," says William. Everyone laughs, including you.

"What else do you see?" you ask to keep everyone focused.

"Although there are many items in the To Do column, there seems to be more in the In Progress column," says Matt.

"And how does what you see make you feel?" you ask.

"Stressed out!" says Roger. Everyone except Ben nods in agreement.

"Relieved!" says Ben. You ask Ben to elaborate. "I could see from everything happening around us that we had too much work in progress, but without visualizing it, it was hard to get everyone to openly acknowledge the seriousness of the situation."

"How are you feeling?" you ask Jason.

Jason is fidgeting with his left ear again. "Lost," he says quietly. "I always knew I had a lot on my plate. Seeing all this makes me realize I'm not sure what we're trying to achieve anymore."

The rest of the team nods in agreement.

"There are days when it feels like we're trapped in a zombie movie," says William as he starts humming the tune to

Michael Jackson's "Thriller." The team explodes with laughter.

Continue with the adventure on page 112.

## Open Questions

"How are we going to get ourselves out of trouble and back on track?" you ask the team.

Ben says, "We need to know where we are and then figure out where we're headed, followed by joining the dots to get from one to the other."

You take a picture of the board as is for later. In addition to being part Socrates, part Sherlock Holmes, and part A-Team, you're also part Jimmy Olsen from Superman. It's your responsibility to record the team's journey of learning so that people can look back and see how far they've come.

"So, how do we visualize where we are?" you ask.

"How about we start by moving everything we're not actively working on back into To Do?" suggests William.

"That doesn't solve the problem that we've got too much work to do for the deadline we've been given," says Roger.

You explain that while what Roger says is true, William's suggestion is a baby step in clarifying the status of the team's work.

You give the team five minutes to update the In Progress column. Ding! goes the bell.

Continue with the adventure on page 113.

# Mission Impossible

Next, you ask the team to list the high-level deliverables in priority order for the release. You have a hunch that the large amount of work in progress is due to a lack of clear priorities.

William starts humming "Thriller" again and, this time, the others join in. Nobody moves.

You repeat the request, this time asking everyone to create a list to the best of their knowledge. After a very long five minutes, the team manages to articulate five key features in the next release.

"They seemed like such great ideas back then," says Nancy.

"They still are," says Ben.

"The problem is that everything is a must-have, and we knew from the beginning that we could never deliver it all by the deadline that was set," says Roger.

"As Scrum master, I should have pushed back harder," says Ben quietly. Ash disagrees, and so do some of the others.

"We all said it was impossible," says William, "but both the business and management didn't want to hear it."

"Our most urgent problem right now is that we've only got three more sprints before the release date," says Ben.

Continue with the adventure on page 114.

# Hope Lives

"I guess that's it for us then," says Jason, throwing his arms up in the air.

Rebecca jumps in. "That's not the way to think about it!" she says. "Let's reestimate the effort for implementing the features again and prioritize them by return on investment. Then we can figure out what we can actually deliver for the release. What we need is to provide at least some value to keep our customers happy. Cassandra will be able to tell us if it's enough."

"Rebecca's right!" says Ash nodding. "We're the Dream Team. There must be something we can deliver to make our customers happy."

"What about the business value of each feature? The business has never been able to provide that," says Ben.

Nancy pitches in. "Between us, we've got lots of shared knowledge about the business. I bet we can come up with a relative business value estimate per feature."

"They would probably be as accurate as our development estimates," says William. This time, no one's laughing.

Continue with the adventure on page 115.

# Numbers

"If I were a superhero, my superpower would be estimation," says Matt. Roger sniggers.

"What problems do you face with estimation?" you ask.

"People complain that we take ages to come up with them," says Ben. "That's because we know that when we release the estimates to the business and management, they become set in stone and we go on a death march for getting the estimates wrong."

"That's because, more often than not, we underestimate," Ash adds. "It's impossible to estimate for things we don't know about at the time of estimating."

"We won't ever be able to change that. The framework has grown too big and too complex for a single team to know it inside and out," sighs Matt.

It's your job to help people think. "How can we improve the accuracy of our estimates?" you ask.

"It's true no one team is an expert on the whole framework," says Roger. "But I bet we'd all be a lot smarter if we got together with other teams and used our collective knowledge and experience to improve our estimates."

After a long silence, Matt says, "We don't have time to waste; let's get started. We'll just have to manage on our own like we've done in the past. Give us sixty minutes, Jim." The rest of the team nods in agreement, while Roger looks disappointed.

"Sure," you reply. You set the timer and your watch to sixty minutes, and then you ding the bell.

It's time for an afternoon stroll.

Continue with the adventure on page 116.

## Sinking Ship

As you walk around the building, your one-on-one conversation with Matt springs to mind.

According to Matt, team members did all the right things when they first started to adopt agile. They brought in a coach to help, with the intention of taking things forward themselves shortly afterward.

"The problem was that when nothing changed, instead of taking a long hard look at ourselves and doing something about it, we changed coaches," said Matt. "You could say we were in denial."

"In the end, not only did our good intentions fall by the wayside, it also seems our company is now crumbling before our eyes," he added.

Matt continued. "Patrick's done the right thing bringing you in to get us back on track and help us stay on track. Depending on your recommendations, we should also look at how we can improve our technical skills to help us make the most of agile. Now I'm worried we haven't hired you in time. It may already be too late to save the company, let alone the team."

Continue with the adventure on page 117.

## Surprise

You take a different route to the break room just for fun. Who should you bump into but Cassandra on her way to a meeting.

"Hi, Jim," she says. "Have you been to see our other agile teams? I'm sure they'd like to meet you. Go up one floor, turn left, and there's a bunch of them just around the corner."

You thank Cassandra and tell her the Dream Team's busy updating and tidying their kanban board.

Cassandra nods and smiles.

Do you:

- pay the teams a visit on page 118, or
- postpone the visit and go for your coffee break on page 121?

# Rainbow Corridor

You go through the dark corridor to discover at least half-a-dozen team spaces covered in sticky notes, photos, technical designs, and user experience storyboards.

To your left are Teams Red, Blue, and Purple. To your right are Teams Yellow, Green, and Orange. You know this because each space is clearly labeled with a team name, next to which are pictures and names of team members on display for everyone to see.

One of the team members from the Green Team notices you wandering around and introduces himself.

"Hi, I'm Owen," says the young man with a shaved head and a firm handshake. "Welcome to the Rainbow Corridor."

"Hi, I'm Jim," you say and smile.

"We all know who you are," says Owen. The other Green Team members look up, smile, and get straight back to work. Owen explains he's the Scrum master and offers you a tour of the team's space.

He tells you that the team is really busy, as they are halfway through the sprint and have just discovered a whole bunch of tasks they didn't realize needed doing at the start of the sprint.

He shows you a sprint burndown chart, with the progress flatlining for the past two days.

You ask a few open questions and within minutes ascertain that the additional work is the result of teams doing cross-program estimating and planning in isolation.

"We've suggested getting a team rep from each team to all meet up for a daily scrum of scrums to improve communication," Owen explains. "It worked at first, but after a couple of days, when the teams started falling behind with their work, everyone just reverted back to working in isolation."

Owen looks weary. "We'd really appreciate some help," he says.

You suggest a chat over coffee.

Continue with the adventure on page 120.

# Systems Thinking

Owen has a double espresso. You opt for a green tea for a change. Owen also orders a double-chocolate muffin.

You happen to catch his eye at the checkout. "My wife thinks I'm comfort eating," he explains. You smile. He chuckles.

The two of you find a table in a quiet corner. You take out your pen, notebook, and a pack of small sticky notes, ready for some systems thinking.

As Owen describes the current situation, you note down each point, one per sticky note. You place them relative to one another in terms of cause and effect. You occasionally shuffle the sticky notes around as you remodel their relationships based on what Owen tells you. Next, you join up the sticky notes with arrows. Sticky notes that represent causes have arrows pointing toward sticky notes that represent effects.

There are a couple of tips you've learned when creating a cause-effect diagram. One, you always iterate over the diagram, because by doing so, you can test the logical reasoning underlying the diagram. Two, you refine the descriptions to reflect the language used by those involved so that the diagram is as meaningful to them as possible.

When Owen finishes talking, you sum up what you've heard based on the diagram that's emerged to validate your understanding.

Continue with the adventure on page 123.

# Calm Before the Storm

You sit down with a cup of coffee and look out into the rain. This time of day, all is still and quiet in the break room.

You take a deep breath in and exhale slowly. As you breathe out, you count to five, and the fog in your mind begins to lift.

You've put yourself in this kind of situation many times before. A team is underperforming and you're called in to help. And yet, no matter how many times you go through this experience, it never ceases to amaze you how much hard work it takes to bring about positive change that endures. The outcome of your engagement, if successful, marks the start of a slow and long journey of change.

You suspect that the reason so many of the team's problems are difficult to solve is because they are systemic. By systemic, you mean they're ingrained in the well-worn fabric that makes up an organization, also known as the "company culture."

Continue with the adventure on page 122.

## Root Cause

The key to getting the team back on track is to first identify the root causes of its problems and then look at what's within the team's scope of control to change on its own and what's not. You know these are the two places where you'll find the options to help the team move forward.

The alternative is to create a plan predicated on a change in culture. Such a lofty goal could be compared to gambling one's entire life savings on the lottery. The cost and risk is simply too high for the likelihood of success on such a large scale. Plus Patrick has made it clear that there's neither the time nor the energy to tackle this massive challenge at this moment in time.

This reminds you of a joke: How do you eat an elephant? One bite at a time.

The most urgent need right now is to figure out how to get the Dream Team back on track. Your approach of using agile techniques to figure out how best to adopt agile has worked well in the past.

By the end of today, you should have the necessary evidence to substantiate the key problems the team faces. You'll end the day by ensuring the team has a draft set of delivery options for this release.

Tomorrow you'll work with the team to validate and confirm the delivery options for moving forward. Then, together, you'll prioritize those options based on value, dependencies, constraints, and risks.

Your cup is now empty and you feel recharged. You take another deep breath in and then exhale slowly to a count of five.

It's time to head back and see how the team's doing.

Continue with the adventure on page 181.

## Cause and Effect

"If I understand correctly, the Green Team is experiencing stress and fatigue because of the large amount of work in progress," you begin. "The more tired people get, the more stressed out they become. And the more stressed out they become, the more tired they get."

You then point to the sticky notes and arrows in the lower right corner of the diagram. "This is a classic example of a vicious circle," you continue. "As you can see, by definition, it's a self-reinforcing feedback loop."

Owen traces a finger around the vicious circle. "That's what I've been trying to say! But unlike you, I sound crazy. Maybe this will help people see what's really happening. Okay, what's causing the huge amount of work in progress?" asks Owen.

You move your finger from the "Lots of WIP" sticky note up the trunk of the tree. "Lack of prioritization. Based on what you've said, everything is a top priority, and none of the stakeholders are prepared to budge on their priorities."

"Too right!" exclaims Owen. "Tell me more."

You nod. "And why can't the requirements be prioritized? For three key reasons: One, the project scope is unclear. Two, we don't know the value of the requirements. Three, we have conflicting requirements. All three causes together make it extremely hard to prioritize. That's a common reason why people stop prioritizing altogether."

Owen nods again. "And that's why the business stakeholders keep asking for all or nothing. That makes it impossible to have conversations about how we can deliver at least some of what they want!"

"Let's continue," you say. "To verify the logic between each of these reasons, we need to ask why. Why is the scope unclear? Why can't we assign value to the requirements? Why do we have conflicting requirements?"

Owen nods as he moves his finger to the top of the tree. He says, "It turns out they all share a common cause because the project goals are unclear. According to this diagram, unclear project goals seem to be the root cause of the Green Team's stress and fatigue."

## *Current Reality Tree*

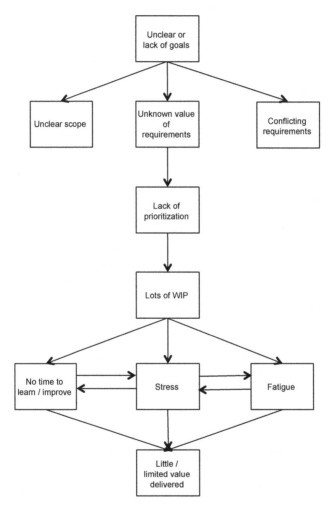

Continue with the adventure on page 125.

# Panic-Driven Development

"That's been the case since the start of the project," says Owen. "A number of us from IT questioned the value of the project from the very beginning, but we were told to simply get on with it and stop asking so many questions."

Owen continues. "Progress stopped because we didn't know where we were headed and why. We got caught up in lengthy arguments between stakeholders about which requirement should be implemented first. We knew we had to do as many as possible. That made us panic, and we ended up trying to work on everything at once."

Owen pauses, gulps down his espresso, and stares at the diagram.

"Don't get me wrong," says Owen. "It's a great diagram. It captures what we already know, but how do we begin to sort things out?"

You explain the diagram is what's known as a cause-effect diagram and, more specifically, a current reality tree.

"If only I could see what the future reality looks like," says Owen, "then I would know how long I've got before I tell my wife I need to look for a new job."

Continue with the adventure on page 126.

## Fortune Telling

"To create a future reality tree, we simply turn things upside down and inside out," you say with a reassuring smile. Owen continues to stare at the current reality tree as though he could will the future into existence.

## *Future Reality Tree*

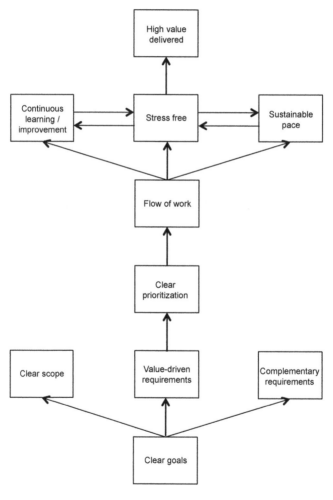

You point to the bottommost row of sticky notes in the current reality tree.

"What if we had clear project goals?" you say while writing out "clear project goals" on a sticky note.

"We'd be able to know what's in scope and, more importantly, what's out of scope," suggests Owen. You write down "clear scope" on another sticky note.

"We'd also be able to, at the very least, assign relative business value to each high-level requirement based on its contribution to the overall project goals," says Owen, who begins to smile. You write down "value-driven requirements" on another sticky note.

"Instead of accepting conflicting requirements, it would become much easier to see which of the conflicting requirements contribute most to our goals," continues Owen. You write down "complementary requirements" on another sticky note.

"What's more, these three factors would enable us to clearly prioritize all the requirements," says Owen, "and to create a steady flow of work for the team. " You write down "clear prioritization" and "flow of work" on two separate sticky notes.

Owen finishes by saying, "And if we had all this in place, the team could work stress-free at a sustainable pace!"

Continue with the adventure on page 128.

## The Big Picture

Now it's Owen's turn to smile.

"I'm beginning to understand what seeing the bigger picture means," says Owen. "We've just described the situation for all the projects I've ever worked on in this company."

Owen pauses, then mutters to himself, "No wonder it feels like we're stuffed."

"How true is that last statement?" you ask.

"Not entirely. I'm beginning to see the light at the end of the tunnel," says Owen. "Correction. You've lit a match and I can now see that we're in a tunnel. Before our conversation, the team and I were just scrambling in the dark."

You tell Owen it's time you checked in with the Dream Team.

"That team's got their fair share of challenges ahead of them," says Owen. "We'll do what we can to help. Meanwhile, what do I do with all this information we've gathered?"

"What do you suggest?" you ask in return.

"A question in response to a question," muses Owen. "You're using the Socratic method. I think you can make a big difference here."

You nod and wait for Owen to answer the question, on page 129.

## Next Stop

"How about I go back and talk through both diagrams with the team?" says Owen. "We can then come up with a small set of actions to help reduce our WIP right away in order to get the team moving again."

You both get up, and Owen gives you a firm handshake. "I really appreciate your time, Jim. I do feel a bit of an idiot for not having seen things more clearly before, but at least now we know which way to go to get out of the tunnel."

"It's always useful to have a thinking buddy," you reply.

The two of you part ways for now. You're glad you could help Owen.

Continue with the adventure on page 130.

# Divide and Conquer

The Dream Team team space is empty when you arrive.

You walk over to the the kanban board to find a list of high-level requirements. Each item is written on an index card and has a relative business value noted down in the lower left corner, while the corresponding effort estimate is in the lower right corner. In between the business value estimate and the effort estimate is a third number, the return on investment (or ROI) of that story, which is calculated by dividing the business value by the effort.

You notice the current list is prioritized by ROI.

After a few minutes, Roger and Ben return.

"We've been working hard," says Roger. He peels the top card off the wall and shows you the mass of yellow sticky notes on the back. "We've even done a task breakdown for the items in order to provide as meaningful an estimate as possible."

"Maybe we'll be agile one day," says Nancy as she returns with a cup of a coffee and a pack of chocolate chip cookies. You all laugh. She offers everyone a cookie.

Continue with the adventure on page 131.

# Estimation Extravaganza

You ask everyone to huddle around for an update. Rebecca offers to start it off.

"We began by collecting as many high-level requirements as possible, then we applied relative estimation to the business value of each requirement in three steps," says Rebecca. "First, we did T-shirt sizing, arranging them from the largest amount of business value to the smallest. Second, we assigned a relative business value estimate to the smallest one, starting with 100. Then we relatively calculated a business value estimate in business value points for the rest of the items."

"Then we used the same process to come up with effort estimates for the items," says Ash. "Since we couldn't agree on the effort estimates as easily as we could on the business value estimates, we broke down the items into development and QA tasks."

"We know that agile estimating separates the size of the work (T-shirt sizes and relative effort estimates) from the rate of working (hours). However, most of us still find it easier to estimate tasks in terms of hours, so we did this for the smallest item," explains William. "That way, we could map a 10-story-point item to 20 hours of effort at a task level and double-check it in a unit we're familiar with."

You make a note to discuss further the benefits of estimating using only story points and not hours at a later date. For now, the most important thing is for the team members to come up with estimates that reflect what they think they can realistically achieve for the release.

"We then used the smallest item like a cookie cutter to double-check our story point estimates," says Ben. "For instance, the next item had an initial effort estimate of 20 story points. After we did the task breakdown for that and estimated the tasks in hours, it turned out to be closer to 15 story points instead of 20."

Ben interjects. "The tasks and hour estimates are used only within the team," he explains. "For us, story points offer a level of abstraction that we use for discussing the cost of a story with the business."

There are a total of twelve items. "How did you manage to do all this in sixty minutes?" you ask.

Ethan explains. "We split into two groups, each with a business analyst or tester plus a few developers. We worked on breaking down and estimating different items and then came back together to share our thoughts and estimates. We also adjusted the individual group estimates based on additional information and insights from the team as a whole."

Last but not least, Jason chips in. "I was surprised by how quickly we managed to do all this. I drifted between the two groups to answer specific questions."

"The process seems to have worked really well," says Ash. You notice that Jason is smiling for the first time.

Continue with the adventure on page 133.

## Next Challenge

"Good job!" you say. The team is smiling and eager to move onto their next challenge.

"Your next and final challenge for the day is to come up with some delivery options," you say. "We have only a few more sprints before the next release. Based on the ROI and value estimates, what are the different groups of features we can release to keep our customers happy?"

"We understand the goal of the challenge," says Matt, smiling. "Can you give us some acceptance criteria?" The team is learning fast.

You say, "By the end of the challenge, we should have at least three options of what we can deliver in the next few sprints, along with a clear list of pros and cons, dependencies, constraints, and risks for each option."

"Don't we need our product owner for this?" interrupts Jason.

"Ideally, yes," you reply. "But since we have limited time with Cassandra, preparing a list of delivery options will help us make the best use of our time with her."

"It's also a good way to test how well we understand the business strategy," adds Rebecca.

"How long have we got?" asks Ethan.

"In the spirit of sustainable pace, let's aim to all leave the office by 5:30 today," you suggest.

"I'm all for sustainable pace!" says William.

"We have sixty minutes. Let's go, team!" says Ben as he sets the timer and dings the bell.

Continue with the adventure on page 134.

# Planning with Purpose

"Where do we begin?" says Jason.

"One way to think about this is to imagine we're going shopping," you suggest. "Figure out what your 'budget' is, the equivalent to your average velocity per sprint. Multiply it by the number of sprints you're planning for, and that's the amount of work you can 'shop' for in story points."

"Let's begin with what we feel would be achievable given our time frame. No wishful thinking!" says Nancy.

"So, what's delivery option number one, our plan A?" asks William.

The team agrees quickly on the items that would make up the first of the three sprints based on the highest ROI possible. Planning work for the second sprint takes a bit longer, while planning the third sprint takes the longest. This is to be expected, since the third sprint is furthest into the future and the team simply doesn't have as much information about that as it does for work in the next immediate sprint.

Next, the team repeats these steps for the second delivery option, plan B. This time, the team decides to plan by highest value possible. Everyone helps write out duplicate story cards with just the story titles that feature in both the first and second plan. There's about a 50 percent overlap in identical stories.

"Some of these higher-value stories still require more analysis, so that makes them harder to estimate accurately," says Roger. "How should we reflect this in the plan?"

"We could reduce the amount of stories we include," says Ben.

"How about we fill up our Plan B with two-thirds of our original estimated sprint velocity?" suggests William. Everyone agrees.

There are lots of different conversations by the time the team decides on its strategy for the third delivery option, Plan C.

The team members select the items they feel most ambitious about in terms of value and effort. Once again, there is some overlap between this plan and plans A and B.

Once they have identified the three options, they revisit each option to create a corresponding list of pros and cons, dependencies, constraints, and risks for each release option.

Continue with the adventure on page 136.

## Offer Options

Within an hour, the Dream Team has produced three different options in the form of alternative release plans with varying amounts of value, ROI, and risk.

OPTION 1—Full Online Self-Service

- BV: 150k, Cost: 240 story points, ROI: 625

- Includes: Arranging meetups, automated meetup reminders by text and email, posting feedback, selective publishing of feedback

- Current functionality: Done manually behind the scenes through an operator interviewing the client and entering information into the system. This has worked well in the past, but as the business grows, it is no longer scalable with same number of operators.

OPTION 2—Partial Online Self-Service with Improved User Tracking

- BV: 50k, Cost: 40 story points, ROI: 1250

- Includes: Arranging meetups only, plus basic web interface for operators to record operator-to-customer interactions

- Current functionality: Meetups arranged manually through an operator interviewing the client and entering information into the system. User activity is recorded using paper files.

OPTION 3—Enhanced Customer Profiling and Recommendations

- BV: ???, Cost: 30 story points, ROI: ???

- Includes: Enhanced customer profile by linking with LinkedIn, Twitter, and Facebook profiles, plus instant customer recommendations sent to a customer

- Current functionality: Does not exist

By this point, everyone looks frazzled.

"Good job," you say. "We've taken our first baby step toward value-driven delivery. Get some rest, and we'll look at these tomorrow with fresh eyes."

"I'm off for a swim," smiles Roger.

"And I'm off to pick up my daughter," says Nancy.

Continue with the adventure on page 138.

# Coach's Log: Day 3

February 3

ACTIVITIES

- Had meeting with Cassandra, Dream Team product owner, for the first time

- Visited the Dream Team team space with Patrick

- Ben talked Patrick through results of the project retrospective

- Met Team Predator, second team to try agile

- Hosted joint team lunch with the Dream Team and Team Predator

- Held exercise with Dream Team members to visualize all their work and update kanban board

- Saw Dream Team come up with a prioritized backlog, including value and effort estimates prioritized by ROI, on its own

- Visited Rainbow Corridor agile teams thanks to Cassandra's suggestion

- Met the Green Team

- Introduced systems thinking to Owen, Scrum master of the Green Team, over coffee break

- Reviewed Dream Team's draft set of delivery options for current release

WHAT WENT WELL

- Learned additional information about the company, such as it going public, from Cassandra's open and frank dialogue with me

- Learned about the company culture from both team members and Cassandra and over joint team lunch conversation

- Reconnected Scrum masters Ben and Rickard and their teams

- Discovered an entire floor filled with six more Scrum teams!

- Helped Owen visualize challenges faced by Green Team and how they can change their current reality through systems thinking

- Delivered lots of coaching value to the organization today

- Am still working at a sustainable pace (just about)

WHAT WENT WRONG

- Not everyone could make it to the joint team lunch because of the short notice.

PUZZLES

- Do I have enough data to substantiate my options for helping the Dream Team move forward?

- Who else can I validate the options with when we have them to ensure they're as robust and appropriate as possible?

IMPROVEMENT ACTIONS

- Remember to take regular breaks as breaks.

- Adjust scope of activities now that I know more about the team's velocity. Overestimated how much we could do this afternoon. Didn't have time to update the kanban board and tidy it up.

DAY RATING: 8.5/10

Continue with the adventure on page 154.

## News Spreads

Day 3, and it's time for your daily catch-up with Patrick.

Before you sit down, Patrick says, "I hear you've caused quite a bit of commotion in the team since your arrival."

You want to explain, but you wait for Patrick to finish.

"'That's why we hired you,' is what I told Jason," says Patrick with a smile.

You update Patrick on the events of yesterday, including how there was a confrontation between Jason and yourself at the start of the project retrospective.

With that out of the way, you don't dwell on the difficulties. Instead, you focus on the options for moving forward.

One way is to get Jason's buy-in before continuing with your information gathering and analysis of the situation with the team. Another option is to proceed with or without Jason. You've been in such situations before. You've learned that giving people like Jason the time and space they need usually benefits everyone involved.

Patrick asks you to invite him to all team activities you have planned so that he can drop by and see for himself how things are going.

There's a knock. Jason's at the door.

Continue with the adventure on page 141.

# Slander

"Morning, Jason," says Patrick as Jason takes a seat next to Patrick and directly opposite you.

"Jim's already filled me in on the team's progress," says Patrick. "Now I'd like to hear what you think."

Jason avoids making eye contact with you.

Addressing only Patrick, Jason launches into a tirade of all the outstanding work the team still has to do for the current release. He questions the value of the numerous meetings you've set up for the team. Jason describes them as a "complete waste of time" and wonders what you hope to achieve out of them that the team can't do by itself.

Continue with the adventure on page 142.

## Treaty

After Jason finishes, Patrick says, "The management team has asked Jim to come up with recommendations to help the team move forward. Based on my understanding of your continued concerns with the team and Cassandra, you would agree that we simply cannot continue with the team as is if we want take our product to the next level."

Jason leans forward to respond, but Patrick holds up his hand and continues. "We hope the recommendations will provide the opportunity for the team to prove they can work together and deliver at least 50 percent of the estimated value based on the original business case for this release. Our company needs this right now if we're serious about going public."

Jason can't remain silent any longer. "I've mentioned a million times that the developers simply do not have the ability to appreciate the intricacies of the in-house framework we've developed. Then there's that woman who claims to understand our customers better than those who created the original product. We don't need to ask customers for their input and feedback to know we're right. That's just a waste of time!"

Patrick remains perfectly composed. "To reiterate," he says, "We have less than three days for Jim to come up with recommendations and we need to know if you're on board with this exercise. Consider this week as a modest additional investment, given how much the current release has already cost us."

Before Jason can respond, Patrick thanks you for your time and tells you he will continue the conversation with Jason in private. Patrick tells you to move forward with the team without further delay.

Continue with the adventure on page 143.

# Desperate Remedies

When you return to the team space, Ben says he's got something important to tell you.

"I overheard Patrick telling one of the managers last week that Love Inc. has a number of options when it comes to the future of software development. They can choose to out-source IT entirely or address the challenges we have one by one, beginning with the Dream Team," Ben says.

According to Ben, management can either keep the team together as is or split the team up and redistribute the people across other teams. Or they could disband all existing teams and shuffle people around in the hope that a change of teams will be enough to reinvigorate everyone and give the orga-nization a morale boost.

"Whichever option they choose, it won't count for much unless they address the root cause of all the problems," Ben tells you.

"In my opinion, the rift between the business and IT has become a chasm. It may be too late to build a bridge to meet each other halfway," he continues.

"One more thing," says Ben. "Patrick said yesterday that he's prepared to wait until after hearing your recommenda-tions before deciding what to do with the team. Whatever management decides to do next with the Dream Team will set a precedent for the entire IT department going forward," says Ben.

Continue with the adventure on page 144.

## Truce

Instead of holding the project retrospective immediately, you inform the team that the meeting will resume after lunch today. You hope this will buy Jason some time to make up his mind about whether or not he'll help the team. This way, if he chooses to stay and help, he won't feel the team has left him behind.

By late morning, Jason returns and tells you he has decided to stay. He mutters he'll do his best to make things work. You notice he says this without looking you in the eye.

Continue with the adventure on page 145.

## Hinder, Not Help

Over the next couple of days, despite Jason's words of collaboration, he continues to challenge everything you do, as well as everything the team suggests. Jason's active resistance, combined with the delay from postponing the project retrospective, has resulted in severe consequences for your five-day schedule.

By the end of the week, the team's exhausted from the constant conflict and resistance. There are daily murmurings of team members looking for new jobs when—not if—their project gets outsourced.

You realize too late that you could have done things differently. Rewind back to Tuesday's project retrospective. Judging from your one-on-one conversations with the individual team members beforehand, it's likely the majority would have voted to continue the meeting had you given them the chance. The meeting would have therefore gone ahead, and Jason's outburst wouldn't have been such a big deal.

Alternatively, after your three-way conversation with Patrick and Jason, you three should have agreed on some concrete actions that would have ensured that Jason helped to get the project back on track instead of getting in the way.

Unfortunately, hindsight is a luxury you can't afford. Patrick and the management team are unimpressed by the rapid deterioration in the team's morale and progress. After your presentation on Friday, they thank you for your time and tell you your services are no longer required.

THE END

## Making Waves

It's Day 3, and it's time for your daily catch-up with Patrick.

Patrick says, "I hear you've caused quite a bit of commotion in the team since your arrival."

You want to explain but wait for him to finish.

"'That's why we hired you,' is what I told Jason," says Patrick with a smile.

You update Patrick on the events of yesterday, including the confrontation between Jason, yourself, and the team. You also tell him that you had a one-on-one conversation with Jason shortly afterward, and it remains unclear if Jason is supportive of what you are trying to achieve.

Nonetheless, you don't dwell on the difficulties. Instead, you focus on the options for moving forward.

One way is to get Jason's buy-in before proceeding with your information gathering and analysis of the situation as a team. Another option is to proceed regardless and leave Jason to decide in his own time. You've been in such situations before, and giving people like Jason the time and the space to think things over can benefit everyone involved.

Patrick asks you to invite him to all team activities you have planned so that he can drop by and see for himself how things are going.

"You've got a tough challenge ahead, but the management team and I support you," says Patrick. "Let's go see the team now, and I'll have a word with Jason."

Continue with the adventure on page 147.

# Checkpoint

When the two of you arrive in the team space, the only people around are Jason and Matt. Those two are the early birds of the team. Patrick greets them both, then offers to buy Jason a coffee.

After they're gone, Matt comes over to your desk. "How are we doing in terms of the schedule for these five days?" he asks.

"We're a day behind the original plan, but there's some slack. So long as we do the project retrospective today, we should still have enough time to come up with a plan to help the team move forward."

Matt seems uncertain and asks you to clarify the scope and success criteria of the work agreed on between you and Patrick.

Continue with the adventure on page 148.

# The Goal

You show Matt the story you and Patrick wrote together for the engagement.

PROVIDE RECOMMENDATIONS

As a management team, we need a list of recommendations so that the Dream Team delivers some value for this release and so that it knows how to improve its team performance over time.

ACCEPTANCE CRITERIA

- Two or more delivery options outlined, each of which provide at least 50 percent of the original business case for the release

- Two or more recommendations for improving team performance

- Measures for gauging improvement in team performance

"The agreement is for me to come up with recommendations to help the team move forward," you say. "If the recommendations are accepted, they should provide the opportunity for the team to deliver at least 50 percent of the estimated value based on the original business case for this release."

Matt looks you straight in the eye and says, "Do you still think all these things are achievable now that you know more about our situation?"

You look right back at him and say, "There's no doubt the requirements contain significant value. The big question is how we can work together to deliver the minimum requirements to satisfy our end customer this quarter." Then you change the subject.

Continue with the adventure on page 149.

## Stay Sharp

"Do you know Aidan from Team Predator?" you ask.

"Sure! He joined a year ago. I voted for us to hire him," says Matt. "Why do you ask?"

You explain you think it would be good for the two of them to spend a bit of time together to exchange their skills, knowledge, and experience. You add that Aidan seems to know a lot about the latest technologies and technical practices that may prove useful to the Dream Team.

Matt goes quiet.

The moment passes, and he says quietly, "I'll see if I can have a word with Aidan before the team gets in."

Before Matt leaves the team space, he turns around and says, "Thanks for the suggestion. Let's hope this old dog isn't too old to learn some new tricks!"

Continue with the adventure on page 150.

## Intervention

You head over to the break room for your usual morning coffee. Patrick and Jason are leaving just as you arrive.

Patrick walks over and asks to have a word with you alone.

"Jason's very upset by your presence," says Patrick.

You aren't surprised to hear this, but nonetheless you feel bad that you have caused Jason discomfort. Being an effective coach is about being sensitive to others without being overemotional.

You take a deep breath and then reply, "I'm prepared to be flexible. I can adapt the way I work based on Jason's feedback."

Patrick says Jason's response is nothing personal. He's reacted like this on a number of occasions with different people who've tried to help the team in the past.

"Leave Jason to me," says Patrick. "He's got a couple of days of holiday carried over from last year that he needs to take this week. Continue with whatever you need to do with the team without Jason. He'll join us on Friday afternoon to hear your findings and recommendations."

Patrick shakes your hand and says, "We're a messed up organization, and I'm glad you're here to help."

Continue with the adventure on page 151.

## Missing Person

By the time you return to the team space, everyone's arrived. You ask the team to gather together. You feel you owe them an explanation. You remind yourself to be respectful to all those involved.

"About Jason," you begin. You notice Rebecca staring down at her feet. After Matt, she's the next closest to Jason, having been part of the original team that started Love Inc.

You continue. "Jason has decided to take a couple of days off while we proceed with the project retrospective and information gathering. He'll be back Friday afternoon to hear our findings and recommendations."

There is a long silence.

Ash is the first and only one to speak. "Let's do our best and come up with something Jason would be proud of," he says. A few people nod in agreement.

"Let's break for ten minutes and reconvene in our meeting room for the project retrospective," you say.

Continue with the adventure on page 152.

# Friendship

During the break, Rebecca reminisces about the years she's been friends with Jason. In fact, he's the one who told her about the job at Love Inc.

"For the past year, he's been telling me how unhappy he is with the team's performance," says Rebecca. "He's even considered leaving the company for good. But I know him better than that. Jason loves the product, and no matter how things appear on the outside, he wants to see it through."

"I know we can be a stubborn and tough crowd sometimes," she continues. "We've developed a bunch of bad habits. Now that the time's come for us to change, some of us are gripped by fear. I've learned the toughest challenge to overcome is our own resistance to change."

Rebecca says she has had to frequently remind Jason that agile is deceptively simple yet incredibly hard to do well because it requires a mindset shift.

According to Rebecca, the new definition of "smart" has agility built in these days. She paraphrases Darwin based on something she's read on agile, "It's not the strongest of the species that survive, nor the most intelligent, but the ones most adaptable to change."

"I only hope we adapt quick enough to keep going," says Rebecca. "We were a team of high achievers once upon a time. I hope we can do it again."

Continue with the adventure on page 153.

# Leopard Spots

Day 3 ends on a higher note than when you started. The project retrospective refocuses the team on their immediate goal of figuring out how to get both the project and the team back on track.

The rest of the week flies by. Before you know it, it's time to present your recommendations. You feel confident they will enable the team to start delivering again.

One of your recommendations is to swap people between the Dream Team and the other agile teams. This will serve to reinvigorate the Dream Team as well as disseminate skills and promote knowledge sharing within the company. Everyone's excited by the recommendation except Jason.

Jason's a classic example of someone who can recite the theory of agile but fails to apply it in practice. You empathize with Jason because you, too, struggle to always apply the agile values and principles yourself, especially when under pressure. Agile demands a person to dig deep and want to change themselves for the better for the greater good.

You've also observed that Jason is tired from working in the same team for so long. As the saying goes, a change is as good as a rest. That's why you've advised Patrick to move Jason into Team Predator, where they're in desperate need of his technical knowledge. That way, Jason and Aidan can enable the team to redesign the existing framework Jason and Matt built.

No matter what happens next, you know that you've had a positive influence on some of the team members. You leave many of them hopeful in spite of the uncertainty that lies ahead.

THE END

## Surprise Visitor

It's Day 4. Another day and a half remaining before you're due to present your recommendations to the management team.

You arrive in the team space earlier than usual. You are surprised to find Cassandra staring at the kanban board.

You glance around the team space and notice it looks significantly tidier. In spite of the large number of sticky notes in the In Progress column, they're now neatly lined up on the wall.

"The pixies were busy last night," you say.

"I can't believe it!" says Cassandra. "No one's ever done this for me before."

"You're welcome," you say. "The team's looking forward to spending more time with you."

"I'll stop by later on this morning to thank them," says Cassandra.

"By then we should have the delivery options ready for the upcoming release," you say.

"See you later," says Cassandra with a smile. "I don't want to be late for my meeting."

Continue with the adventure on page 155.

## Be Prepared

Patrick is on the phone when you arrive for your daily catch-up. He signals for you to wait.

While you wait, you review your tasks for today.

It begins with a team review of the delivery options from yesterday, followed by Cassandra's weekly hour with the team, where she can review and prioritize the options herself. The rest of the day will involve refining the effort estimates for each option and finalizing the Dream Team's proposed release plan.

You've come a long way since Monday morning. You now have a much clearer understanding of the situation thanks to the team's help, as well as Cassandra's. Also, insights from members of the other agile teams have helped you better understand the wider company culture.

Patrick waves you in.

Continue with the adventure on page 156.

## Lightning Update

"Morning, Jim," says Patrick as he mutes his teleconference line. "I've just been pulled into another meeting. What do I need to know?"

You tell Patrick you're making good progress with the team's help and that you will have the presentation ready for tomorrow afternoon. You mention the team would like to attend that meeting.

"I'll get back to you on that," says Patrick as he returns to his teleconference call.

You find yourself standing in the corridor, faced with the day ahead.

Do you:

- prepare yourself for the day on page 157, or
- head back to the team space on page 160?

## Progress Check

You find a quiet place at the back of the cafeteria to think. It's always quiet here early in the morning.

You revisit the user story you wrote with Patrick for this engagement.

PROVIDE RECOMMENDATIONS

As a management team, we need a list of recommendations so that the Dream Team delivers some value for this release and so that it knows how to improve its team performance over time.

ACCEPTANCE CRITERIA

- Two or more delivery options outlined, each of which provide at least 50 percent of the original business case for the release

- Two or more recommendations for improving team performance

- Measures for gauging improvement in team performance

The first and seemingly most risky criteria is in progress. The team has identified some delivery options that are estimated to provide a substantial amount of the original business case for the release. The planning session with Cassandra should confirm the estimated value of the different delivery options.

The second criteria can be derived from the root causes of the team's challenges. Since the Dream Team's challenges are very similar to those encountered by the Green Team, you may be able to use some of the work you've already done with Owen on this.

The third criteria is best done as a team exercise, ideally including Cassandra and perhaps even Patrick, to get both a common understanding of what team performance looks like and to get buy-in on how to measure it. Whether or not you do this depends on the team's availability and the time you have before the presentation.

It's the start of Day 4, and you are happy with the progress you've made so far. You plan to begin compiling your recommendations report early this afternoon so that you have time to test and rehearse it before the presentation to the management team tomorrow afternoon.

Continue with the adventure on page 159.

## Still To Dos

Next, you review your work remaining for the presentation tomorrow.

TO DOs

- Identify, evaluate, and prioritize delivery options with Cassandra and the team
- Create list of people/process/technology recommendations
- Produce draft of the presentation
- Rehearse the presentation

There's still quite a lot to do. You always knew a five-day time box would be a challenge. "Sustainable pace," you mutter to yourself.

Continue with the adventure on page 160.

## Nervous Wreck

You return to the team space to find everyone's arrived for the day. You ask the team to gather together.

"Good morning, all. What else do we need to do in preparation for the delivery options walk-through this morning with Cassandra?" you ask the team.

"We've done as much as we can," says Ben.

You notice a certain tension in the air. You decide to change your style of questioning. "How do we feel about it?" you ask.

There's a moment of silence. Ash is the first to answer. "To be honest, I'm a bit afraid of Cassandra. We've tried to make suggestions to her before, but each time she's told us to stick to what we know instead of meddling with the business."

Heads nod around the room.

You nod to show you understand what the team's telling you. You say, "Let's reconvene at ten o'clock for the release replanning meeting."

You know the team's done its best. You plan to go into the meeting with an open mind.

Continue with the adventure on page 161.

## Fresh Start

At precisely ten o'clock, Cassandra arrives in the team space. She begins by thanking the team for tidying up the board and team space.

"We've also cleared a desk for you," says Ben. "Team Predator's product owner sits with the rest of the team twice a week, and it's helped improve communication and the quality of their deliverables significantly," he adds.

Cassandra nods and says, "Let's get on with the planning, shall we?"

Continue with the adventure on page 162.

## Address to Impress

The team has been rehearsing the planning session since yesterday.

Ben gets the ball rolling. "Let's run through the agenda for our planning session," he says. He talks through the agenda in the form of sticky notes. "We'll present and discuss the three options we've come up with for the original target release date, spending up to fifteen minutes per option. We'll finish off by selecting an option and agreeing on a release plan."

"I'm feeling more confident already," says Cassandra with a smile. People have remarked that Cassandra doesn't smile often, at least not at work.

Continue with the adventure on page 163.

## Options, Options, Options

Next, Ash explains the information provided for each of the three options. "Each option consists of a bunch of information: the goal and the estimated business value relative to the other options; the cost, also known as the effort estimate; and the return on investment, as well as the risks associated with that option. We've also provided the pros and cons of each option," he says.

Nancy, Rebecca, and William stand by the flip chart and take turns unveiling one option after another, pausing at the end of each option to answer questions.

OPTION 1—Full Online Self-Service

- BV: 150k, Cost: 240 story points, ROI: 625

- Includes: Arranging meetups, automated meetup reminders by text and email, posting feedback, selective publishing of feedback

- Current functionality: Done manually behind the scenes through an operator interviewing the client and entering information into the system. This has worked well in the past, but as the business grows, it is no longer scalable with same number of operators.

OPTION 2—Partial Online Self-Service with Improved User Tracking

- BV: 50k, Cost: 40 story points, ROI: 1250

- Includes: Arranging meetups only, plus basic web interface for operators to record operator-to-customer interactions

- Current functionality: Meetups arranged manually through an operator interviewing the client and entering information into the system. User activity is recorded using paper files.

OPTION 3—Enhanced Customer Profiling and Recommendations

- BV: ???, Cost 30 story points, ROI ???

- Includes: Enhanced customer profile by linking with LinkedIn, Twitter, and Facebook profiles, plus instant customer recommendations sent to a customer

- Current functionality: Does not exist

Continue with the adventure on page 165.

## Show Me the Money!

When William finishes describing option 3, he asks Cassandra, "What do you think is the business value of this option in comparison with the other two options?"

Cassandra has a poker face. Then she says quietly, "Where did this option come from? I certainly didn't put those features into the backlog."

You notice some of the team members cringe and take a step back. You give Ben the nod.

"Actually, they're a combination of Aidan's and William's suggestions," replies Ben. "They've both been trying out ReadyLove's service, since it's our biggest competitor. That's how we know our customers might want these features."

"That's very dedicated of you both," says Cassandra, turning to William before finally breaking into a big smile. "I'll have to double-check my estimate with marketing, but I reckon it's worth at least as much as option 2. Possibly between 50 and 70k. If we beat ReadyLove in terms of time-to-market for profiling and recommendations, it could be worth even more to us."

You suggest a ten-minute break. Everyone looks relieved, and Cassandra gives Alice from marketing a call.

Continue with the adventure on page 166.

## Respond to Change

When everyone returns from the break, Cassandra is the first to address the whole team.

"Thank you for all your hard work," begins Cassandra. "I know the past nine months haven't been easy for any of us. The options you showed me this morning are impressive. Who would have thought IT could be so innovative? As for the value of option 3, Alice and I have to do a bit more digging around to estimate its business value. We'll have the figures by this afternoon. Let's finish our release planning session then."

Ben turns to check that you agree with changing around the day's agenda. Cassandra notices.

"To double-check my understanding of agile," says Cassandra, "'responding to change' remains more important than 'following a plan' I believe?"

You nod. "Of course," says Ben. Now it's his turn to smile. "This afternoon we'll agree on the high-level scope of the release. Then we'll refine the exact details as part of product backlog refinement prior to planning for each sprint. The stories will need to have clear, testable acceptance criteria before we plan them into a sprint."

"Thanks, everyone," says Cassandra. "I'll be back with Alice around 2 p.m. today."

Continue with the adventure on page 167.

## Team Buzz

The team cheers when Cassandra is out of earshot.

"Did that really just happen?" asks Matt stumbling around, pretending he's about to faint.

"There may still be a way out of our nightmare after all," says Ash as he lets out a sigh of relief. Ash had confided in you about the team's reputation at Love Inc. He feels ashamed that people refer to the team as Team Nightmare instead of by its proper name.

"What do we do next?" asks Jason. This is one of the most positive responses from Jason since you arrived.

Ben looks at you and then at the team. "How about we refine our estimates and reevaluate the risks until lunchtime?" he says.

"It's not every day we get to do some real release planning, so we might as well give it our best shot," says William.

"Remember, an estimate is still an estimate!" says Roger with a slight smile.

You set the timer for sixty minutes.

Do you:

- hang around the team space on page 168, or
- go for a stroll on page 169?

## Rise from the Ashes

While the team divides up into subgroups and people take turns reviewing one another's estimates, you review the list of risks and questions associated with each of the delivery options.

You recognize the rise and fall of excited voices around you as the sound of self-organization.

As you look around the team space, you notice the remarkable transformation that has taken place this week. Without any fanfare, the team has shifted from Tuckman's storming stage to the norming stage in a matter of days. Sometimes such a transition can take groups months or even years. Or it may never happen at all.

The increased focus on shipping the next release has brought team members back together in spite of their differences. There's one thing everyone agrees on: to make the next version of the flagship product something they're all really proud of.

Continue with the adventure on page 243.

# Green Fingers

You decide to go for a stroll along Rainbow Corridor to see how things are going with the Green Team.

When you arrive, Owen smiles and says, "Just the man we were looking for." The team members look up momentarily, nod politely, and then get straight back to work.

On the wall are two flip charts, supersized versions of the current reality tree and the future reality tree you and Owen created together.

"The Green Team's been thinking a lot about continuous improvement since you and I last talked," says Owen. "The plan is to use the two diagrams as our roadmap for continuous improvement. We've identified at least one improvement action for each problem on the current reality tree. We've used green sticky notes to represent improvement actions."

You nod and Owen continues. "As the improvement actions get done, we expect to see things improve. When we achieve one of the sticky notes on the future reality tree, we'll add a picture of an apple to that tree as a fun way to show how much we're really improving."

"Whose idea was it to turn the future reality tree into a fruit tree?" you ask.

One of the developers comes over and introduces himself. "Hi, I'm Brian. The guys wanted to make continuous improvement more fun, so I suggested drawing fruit. It doesn't have to be just apples, we can have all sorts of fruits." A couple of the other developers snigger, and Brian goes back to work.

"We've decided to plan and track our improvement actions as part of every sprint going forward. The team's also committed to setting aside 10 percent of the sprint to do this. Our product owner was reluctant to agree at first, but we're beginning to understand that we need to slow down to go faster," says Owen with a big smile.

Continue with the adventure on page 170.

## See the Bigger Picture

You take a closer look at the future reality tree. It looks like a flourishing tree, while the current reality tree looks withered and gnarly. You're reminded of the power of metaphors.

"That's some fancy artwork," you say with a smile.

"Brian, Jess, and Andy did most of the drawing," says Owen.

You ask Owen for permission to take a picture of the diagrams.

"Sure," says Owen. "I was thinking of inviting the Dream Team around to see if they'd find any of our ideas useful. When I got home last night, all I could think of was how the two trees pretty much sum up all the things that are wrong with projects at Love Inc. They also showed me what the future could look like if we all worked together."

You thank Owen for his offer of help. You mention that the Dream Team is currently busy refining estimates for their delivery options.

"We heard," says Owen. "We might have some information to help de-risk option 3."

Rebecca had warned you that news travels at the speed of Cupid's arrow around here.

"How about you join us for lunch, and you can have a chat with the team about it then?" you say.

"I'll see if I can convince the rest of the team to come along," says Owen. "'Wisdom of crowds,' right? The knowledgeable many can be as smart, if not smarter, than the expert few."

"And the more the merrier! See you at noon in the cafeteria," you say.

Continue with the adventure on page 171.

## Eat, Play, Work

At noon, you make your way over to the cafeteria.

You nod and smile as you sit down with your tray of lasagna and garlic bread. Nothing like a filling lunch for the demanding afternoon ahead.

The whole of the Dream Team sits around two tables deliberately put together.

"Looks like a full house today," you say. "What's the special occasion?"

"It's good to have rest days when you're training hard," says Roger with a serious look on his face, while the rest of the team laughs.

"It's been a long week, and I'm not sick of the sight of you all yet!" says William with a smile as he waves a fist at everyone.

Continue with the adventure on page 172.

## Lunch Party

Ben looks up and says, "Look out for the latecomers!"

"Hey guys, room for a small one?" says Aidan with a wink. Aidan has brought Team Predator with him.

People stand up and drag over another table to make room for the new arrivals.

Then Aidan says, "Looks like we're going to need an extra table." Aidan waves Owen over. Owen has brought along a couple of developers from the Green Team.

It turns out that Owen talked to Aidan after speaking with you during the morning break. Owen thinks that the combined experience of the Green Team and Team Predator may come in handy for estimating some of the Dream Team's upcoming release delivery options.

"We could have a quick chat over lunch to figure out who could help," suggests Aidan.

"And just in case, both our teams have also set aside a bit of time immediately after lunch to go through the delivery options in more detail with your team, if you'd like," says Owen.

Continue with the adventure on page 173.

## Progress

Judging by the noise around the lunch tables, it seems that everyone's having a good time.

"How's the team doing?" Aidan asks you.

"Our session with Cassandra went well," you reply. "We're now waiting for the business value estimates for a new option from the team."

"And how are you doing?" continues Aidan.

"It's been a busy week," you reply.

Aidan leans over and says in a whisper, "We've heard about the work you've been doing with the team and we're impressed. You've lasted longer than the coach before you. Not to mention you've managed to get the team pulling in the same direction!"

You're happy to hear Aidan say this. It's only now that you realize how nervous you really feel about tomorrow's presentation. "With great power comes great responsibility," mutters the voice in your head.

It's time to get back to work.

Continue with the adventure on page 174.

## Better Late Than Never

As you get up to go, Ben says, "A couple of people from Aidan and Owen's teams are going to review our effort estimates before Cassandra returns. This will make our estimates much more robust, for sure. I only wish we'd asked them for help sooner."

You nod and smile.

"The thing about agile," says Ben, "is that it's one thing to talk about collaboration, it's another to do it. As Scrum master to the team, I haven't been leading by example."

"Many ideas in agile sound simple. I find they're anything but easy in practice," you reply.

Continue with the adventure on page 176.

# Agile Fragile

At first, Jason looks a bit awkward among the other team members, but he soon becomes engrossed in a conversation with Ash about the latest open source version control systems.

The rest of the team members are talking about different things, ranging from holidays to ways of making work more fun and interesting.

"That's one of the main reasons I prefer agile to other project methodologies," says William. "It has fun built into many of its practices. You've got things like estimation poker and the release and sprint planning game. Then there are all the different kinds of retrospectives you can run to keep the team fresh and motivated about continuous improvement."

"If that's true, then why did we stop applying agile to the way we work?" blurts out Roger. He's red in the face, and his fists are clenched.

"That's the same question I've been asking myself," replies William quietly, as others around the table nod.

"Agile may sound simple and even fun, but it's not easy," you say. "It requires hard work, discipline, and a collaborative style that can be exhausting when you practice it day in day out."

"Just because something's difficult doesn't mean you should give up," continues Roger.

Ben puts his hand on Roger's shoulder and says, "I think we're all finally coming around to that point of view."

It's time for the team to get back to work.

Continue with the adventure on page 194.

## Drama

When everyone returns to the team space, they seem to be both in high spirits and nervous at the same time.

"How do we feel about the upcoming planning session?" you ask.

"Just the other day, I heard 'drama' being defined as 'a combination of anticipation and uncertainty put together,'" says Nancy. "That's kind of what I'm seeing here, and that makes me feel nervous."

Ethan, the quiet one in the team, says, "Option 3 is what we need to prove our value to the company. It's our chance to change the way people look at us."

"When faced with uncertainty, we can only do our best and keep our options open," you say.

William begins to hum Michael Jackson's "Thriller," and everyone begins to laugh and look more relaxed.

Just then, Cassandra arrives with Alice.

Continue with the adventure on page 177.

# Old Habits Die Hard

The team's laughter is silenced by their visitors' stony faces.

"We've discussed the delivery options with marketing and have had to also consult with Patrick," begins Cassandra. "We now have an even greater challenge for you."

"We want both options 1 and 3," announces Alice.

"But that's impossible!" says Roger. "We'd have to work crazy hours to get it done in time. And even then, we wouldn't make it!"

Matt backs Roger up. "We all know what happens to people and quality when we don't work at a sustainable pace," he says slowly.

Ben tries to move the conversation forward by focusing on the facts. "Our average sprint velocity is 15 points. We have only 3 sprints left before the release date. That's a maximum of 45 points we can realistically plan for if we want a successful release."

"Based on our data, that means we can either deliver option 2 or option 3, but not both 1 and 3," says William.

"We definitely want both options," insists Cassandra. "Together, they provide the minimum scope that would increase our operational efficiency and make us sufficiently desirable to investors."

Do you:

- wait and see what happens next on page 178, or
- intervene on page 182?

## Street Fight

"No one dare mention 'wishful thinking,'" blurts out Cassandra. "I'm sick and tired of this. Every time we ask IT for something, we always get shortchanged. It's a miracle we remain wishful."

The team now feels under attack. Again. Not only is the team being asked to deliver six times the amount of work in comparison with their average historical velocity, the team perceives Cassandra's blatant disregard for quality as the cause for many of the problems in the past that have resulted in the technical debt they continue to have to pay for today.

"How many times do we have to tell you?" says Roger, his voice getting louder with every word he utters. "We don't do magic. We build software. We could try to implement everything you ask for, but we'll have to cut corners. And each time we compromise on quality, we're cutting off our own noses to spite our faces."

Continue with the adventure on page 179.

## Angry Mob

As the saying goes, what's been said cannot be unsaid. What's more, Jason and a couple of the others use this opportunity to let the business really know what they think of the requirements and the nonsense they've had to endure to date.

Emotions are running high, and before you know it, the meeting has spiraled out of control. Cassandra and Alice storm off, promising to escalate the incident to Patrick and the rest of the management team.

Patrick appears within minutes to calm the team down.

Continue with the adventure on page 180.

## History Repeats Itself

The rest of the week flies by. Before you know it, it's time to present your recommendations to the management team. In spite of the argument during planning between Cassandra, Alice, and the team, you feel confident the recommendations will enable the team to start delivering again. Nonetheless, you can't help but wonder if it's a case of too little too late.

You emphasize that planning more work into a release than the team can confidently deliver is likely to jeopardize the entire release. To increase the chances of success, you recommend planning based on the team's historical velocity instead of on wishful thinking. You also reiterate the importance of working at a sustainable pace because that, in turn, increases the predictibility and quality of a release.

Your only wish now is that you'd intervened earlier and said all this before the planning discussion turned ugly. Sometimes, all it takes to resolve a conflict is to keep people listening to each other just long enough to come up with a solution together.

It's now up to the team, Cassandra, and management to agree on the scope and the plan for the upcoming release. Something in your gut tells you that you all have a very long journey ahead.

THE END

# Missed Opportunity

In spite of your best intentions, the rest of the week disappears before your eyes. You thought you had drawn the necessary conclusions about the Dream Team's situation, yet progress with the Dream Team is slower than you expected.

You end up rushing to get the presentation done and only manage to make recommendations local to the Dream Team. You can't help but feel you're missing a huge opportunity to make things better. What's more, the management team isn't impressed by your recommendations.

"You say that we should have clearer project goals and provide value estimates for our requirements so that we can prioritize more effectively and efficiently," says Hugh, the head of marketing and Cassandra's manager. "If those are such big problems, why do all the other teams manage to deliver, while the Dream Team continues to fail time after time?"

It's possible the other teams are too afraid to speak up and work all hours to get releases into production, just like the Dream Team. The only difference may be that the Dream Team has had so many issues compounded over time that they can no longer muddle through, unlike the other teams.

Had you taken up Cassandra's suggestion to visit Rainbow Corridor, you would have been able to substantiate your hypothesis. By framing your recommendations in terms of the bigger picture, you could have explained to the managers why things are the way they are. Maybe you could have even helped trigger positive change for the company as a whole. Instead, the management team decides to set your suggestions aside until they have a clearer understanding of the Dream Team's situation. They thank you for your time and wish you all the best with your next client.

THE END

## Clash

You remind yourself that when things are unclear, it's better to focus on facts and clarify with a question rather than to respond based on assumptions.

"Let's go back to Ben's point. We know that the team's average sprint velocity is 15 points. What do you suggest?" you ask Cassandra.

"Patrick is going to give us both the Dream Team and Team Predator to get this job done," explains Cassandra, "on the condition that the teams agree the work can be divided up between them."

Cassandra continues. "We understand that some things can't be done more quickly even when more people are working on it. All we're looking for are ways to meet the deadline."

Continue with the adventure on page 183.

# Friends to the Rescue

Just then, Aidan and Owen appear, along with a couple of their respective team members.

"Patrick suggested we come over to see how we can help," says Aidan.

Ben explains the situation. Aidan and the new arrivals listen attentively. The two groups then exchange a few questions and answers.

"I know it's sometimes seen as bad practice to compare sprint velocities between teams, Jim," says Aidan. "But we know from experience that one story point roughly equates to the same amount of effort and complexity among our three teams."

"I consider it bad practice only if velocity comparison is used to make teams compete against one another," you reply. "It's common for effective teams working on the same codebase to come to a shared understanding of what one point means to individual teams."

Aidan then confirms Team Predator's average sprint velocity is 18. "Even if we can divide up the work between two teams, our combined velocity for three sprints gives us only 99 points to plan for," he says. "We need at least three times that many points to deliver both option 1 and option 3 as the effort estimates stand."

You intervene and say, "We need more time before an informed decision can be made. Cassandra, when do you need to know whether or not the work can be distributed across the Dream Team and Team Predator?"

"Ideally this afternoon," replies Cassandra. "Patrick wants to know as soon as possible to minimize the delay on getting started."

"Here's what I propose we do," you say. "Together with Aidan and Owen, the team will spend the next couple of hours validating the effort estimates for all three options. We'll then come up with a proposal on how to deliver as much value in the upcoming release as possible by 4 p.m. today. We will succeed if we keep an open mind and not limit ourselves to the current delivery options."

Cassandra looks disappointed but eventually nods. "That would be much appreciated," she says.

Continue with the adventure on page 185.

## Division of Labor

By adopting an open and calm approach to the dialogue with Cassandra, the team has managed to have a constructive conversation, even though there's now even more pressure on the Dream Team to deliver.

Ethan turns to you and says, "What do we do now? We all agree that there's no way we can deliver both options 1 and 3."

You ask for a volunteer to note down the next steps for the team. Nancy moves over to the flip chart in a flash, pen in hand. "Ready," she says.

First, you reiterate the facts by looking at velocity.

- The Dream Team's remaining release velocity = 3 x 15 = 45 points

- Team Predator's remaining release velocity = 3 x 18 = 54 points

- Combined remaining release velocity = 99 points

Next, you ask the team to come up with some new delivery options. Nancy writes all this down while you facilitate.

- Option 4: option 2 + 3 = 70 points

- Option 5: option 2 + parts of option 1 = 99 points

- Option 6: option 3 + parts of option 1 = 99 points

It turns out that the work involved to implement option 4 (options 2 and 3) can be easily divided up between the two teams, while the dependencies of options 5 and 6 are likely to be more complex, depending on which parts of option 1 are to be included.

Continue with the adventure on page 186.

## The Show Must Go On

You continue. "Given the information we have, I suggest we spend our time reviewing the estimates for option 4, and we reuse part of them for options 5 and 6."

Then you ask for a show of hands if everyone thinks they can reestimate option 4 in its entirety in time for the meeting with Cassandra. Everyone agrees it's doable.

"But what about options 5 and 6?" says Roger. "We need Cassandra to agree on which requirements to bundle in before we can estimate."

You explain that since Cassandra isn't available to provide more information right now, all the team can do is make progress by focusing on option 4.

"I agree with Jim," says Ben. "Minimize the work in progress in order to increase focus, which, in turn, will take us closer to our goal!"

Continue with the adventure on page 187.

# One for All and All for One

Everyone agrees that consulting at least some of the Green Team members during estimation will make the estimates more robust, given their deep knowledge of certain parts of the codebase. Meanwhile, Aidan and Owen set off to bring back a few more of their team members to help.

The Dream Team members are happy to get on with the task, so you leave them to it. You set the timer to ninety minutes to get things started. This will give you all thirty minutes to review how far the team has gotten with the task before Cassandra returns.

You email Patrick to find out if the Dream Team could attend your presentation on Friday afternoon. You outline the benefits of the team's attendance, such as including everyone involved and getting their buy-in, as well as providing access to information firsthand.

Within minutes, you receive an updated invite to Friday's meeting from Patrick's personal assistant. You notice she's extended the invite to include everyone from the Dream Team.

Continue with the adventure on page 188.

# Options for Success

After ninety intense minutes, members from the Dream Team, Team Predator, and the Green Team have come up with estimates for option 4. Some of the estimates have gone up, while others have gone down, with the overall total remaining the same.

Cassandra returns to the team space at 4 o'clock with Patrick. Patrick says he wants to see how the team's doing. Cassandra is surprised to see so many options.

You explain, "We've chosen to take an options-based approach so that we can group requirements into bundles with the highest possible value. Each option is based on the information we have right now, each consisting of an estimated value and a cost. We can then figure out which will give us the greatest chance of a successful delivery with the highest possible value."

"Like Jim says, given the limited information we had at the time of estimating, the estimates are subject to significant change," adds Roger.

"But don't we need to have all the final estimates before we can make a decision?" asks Cassandra as she grimaces.

Continue with the adventure on page 189.

# Last Responsible Moment

Instead of giving an answer, you ask an open question. "Let's ask a different question," you say. "When do we need to decide by?"

"By the time we start the next sprint," suggests Ben.

"That makes it first thing next Monday," says Matt.

"I suppose that gives us time to go through the requirements together for options 5 and 6 tomorrow morning," says Cassandra. She looks to Patrick, and he nods.

Cassandra continues, "I'll reschedule my meetings so that I can be with the team from nine to twelve o'clock tomorrow. Will that help?"

"Definitely!" say William and Roger together.

Once this decision-making approach has been agreed on, the team talks Cassandra through the details of option 4. While it isn't the business's first choice based on Cassandra's input this morning, option 4 is achievable given the tight time frame and carries a lot less risk then options 5 and 6 currently do.

"It feels strange yet satisfying that we don't have to make the decision today," says Cassandra.

"It's a great example of the agile principle of postponing important decisions until the last responsible moment," says Ben.

"And every time we find ourselves rushing, we should slow down," adds William.

This makes Matt laugh. "Just as long as we don't end up procrastinating!" he says, voicing the thought that's going through many people's minds at that moment.

Continue with the adventure on page 190.

# A Marathon, Not a Sprint

It's been a long day.

"Thanks for everyone's extra hard work today," says Patrick. "I'm here to help as and when you need blockers removed."

As you look around the room, you notice it's the first time you've seen so many smiling faces at once on the same project.

You remind everyone of the principle of sustainable pace. You encourage everyone to get a good night's rest in preparation for tomorrow.

Continue with the adventure on page 191.

## Unsustainable Pace

Sustainable pace is much easier said than done. Given the turn of events at work, you now have to work late. You call your girlfriend to let her know you have to cancel your movie date. She tells you she was looking forward to seeing you tonight.

It's not the first time you've had to let her down because of work. By now, you recognize the tone of disappointment in her voice, but you don't want to let Patrick and the team down by not being ready for tomorrow's presentation.

Before making your way home to a microwave meal for one, you write your daily log entry.

Continue with the adventure on page 192.

# Coach's Log: Day 4

February 4

ACTIVITIES

- Had morning planning session with Cassandra

- Reviewed engagement goals

- Caught up with Owen about next steps for the Green Team

- Had lunch with the team plus some of Team Predator and the Green Team

- Held afternoon planning session with Cassandra, Patrick, and team, including members from Team Predator and the Green Team

WHAT WENT WELL

- Clear presentation of delivery options to Cassandra from the team

- Super-sociable lunch among the three teams

- A proper team lunch: everyone from the Dream Team was present at lunch—result!

- Aidan and Owen to the rescue with their offer of help for work distribution options

- At second planning session, exceptional teamwork from all three teams, all pulling in the same direction

WHAT WENT WRONG

- The team's initial fear-based reaction toward Cassandra in the morning planning session

- The planning session overran, which means less time to prepare for tomorrow's presentation

- Canceled movie date with Emily because of work

PUZZLES

- What's the likelihood of a successful release delivery from two teams who've never worked together before on the same project?

- What's the best way to manage the work for the release given the tight time frame?

- How do I ensure I work and live at a sustainable pace?

IMPROVEMENT ACTIONS

- Too tired to come up with any for today—I'm sure there are some!

DAY RATING: 6/10

Continue with the adventure on page 195.

## Embrace Uncertainty

By the time the team returns to the team space, everyone seems to be more at ease with each other.

"Just the other day, I heard 'drama' being described as anticipation and uncertainty put together," says Nancy. "That's kind of what I'm seeing here, and that makes me feel nervous."

Ethan, usually the quiet one in the team, says, "Option 3 is what we need to prove our value to the company. It's our chance to change the way people look at us."

William begins to hum Michael Jackson's "Thriller," and everyone begins to laugh and look more relaxed.

Just then, Cassandra arrives with Alice.

Continue with the adventure on page 177.

# Memory Lane

It's Day 5, the last day of your engagement with the Dream Team. You and Patrick have agreed not to meet this morning because you'll be meeting this afternoon.

You reflect on your time with the Dream Team by revisiting the various agile team spaces around the office.

You begin the tour at the Dream Team's team space and then head over to Team Predator's team space. You recall being struck by the differences between the two teams during your early encounters.

The first fundamental difference was their contrasting attitudes toward adopting agile, from Team Predator's "learning agile" philosophy to the Dream Team's approach of abandoning agile because team members already knew it all.

The second most striking difference is team dynamics. Whereas Team Predator consisted of individuals playing on the same side, the Dream Team was no more than a group, a collection of people who happened to sit together at work every day.

In your experience, the difference between a team and a group is that while a team pulls in the same direction toward a common goal, a group pulls in different directions, often going nowhere or until things come apart.

Last but not least, you walk over to Rainbow Corridor, home to half a dozen agile teams. Although you didn't meet all the teams, you did strike up a friendship with Owen, Scrum master of the Green Team. Seeing the challenges the Green Team is up against reminds you that nobody exists in isolation. According to systems thinking, everyone and everything that exists at Love Inc. are all part of the same system. They all impact and are impacted by one another.

Continue with the adventure on page 196.

## Early Birds

By the time you're back at the Dream Team's space, Nancy, Ash, Ben, William, Ethan, and Rebecca have arrived.

"You're all in bright and early this morning!" you say with a smile.

"We've got a big day ahead," says William.

"My husband and I swapped nursery runs this morning so that I could get in a bit earlier," says Nancy. "I didn't want to miss a thing."

"I was in such a hurry, I nearly ran over my neighbor's cat," jokes Ben.

Then Ash says, "I was just telling the others how we seem to have gotten to know each other much better in the past four days than we have in the last six months."

Heads nod around the room.

"We probably want to pace ourselves. We don't want to get sick and tired of each other before we deliver the release," says William, chuckling.

Continue with the adventure on page 197.

# Warm Welcome

Just then, Cassandra arrives with François, Team Predator's product owner. François is carrying a bunch of boxes.

"I didn't know what you guys like for breakfast, so I've brought a mix," says François. "We have muffins, doughnuts, and croissants!"

"Looks like we might all have to go to the gym at lunchtime," says Roger with a smile. You notice that Roger seems more relaxed than you've ever seen him.

"But then we'd miss out on all those deep and meaningful conversations," says William.

Continue with the adventure on page 198.

## Unity

"Grab a pastry and let's get started," says Cassandra. "I've got until midday to answer all your questions regarding options 5 and 6. I've invited François because he's an expert on customer data analysis. He's also here to help me learn to become a better product owner."

"Before we start, how about we clarify our goals for today?" says Ben as he turns to the flip chart poster of the user story for your engagement.

Ben continues. "To estimate options 5 and 6, we need to get the requirements clarified. We also need to help Jim to help us by completing the user story of his engagement."

PROVIDE RECOMMENDATIONS

As a management team, we need a list of recommendations so that the Dream Team delivers some value for this release and knows how to improve its team performance over time.

ACCEPTANCE CRITERIA

- Two or more delivery options outlined, each of which provides at least 50 percent of the original business case for the release

- Two or more recommendations for improving team performance

- Measures for gauging improvement in team performance

You say, "We don't have much time, so let's divide this up. We can reuse the content from this morning's session for the first acceptance criteria. Meanwhile, I can prepare the material to meet the rest of the criteria."

Continue with the adventure on page 199.

# To Dos

Everyone agrees on the plan. Before you go, you facilitate the creation of the session backlog for the next three hours. You also help create a temporary kanban board to ensure the team stays focused and does only what's needed.

Together you write out the goal and come up with the following tasks, one per sticky note:

THE GOAL

Two or more delivery options outlined, each of which provides at least 50 percent of the original business case for the release

TASKS

- Option 5: Clarify scope and requirements sufficiently so the team can provide estimates

- Option 6: Clarify scope and requirements sufficiently so the team can provide estimates

- Option 4: Review option and reestimate based on new or revised information

- Option 5: Estimate

- Option 6: Estimate

"Who'd like to facilitate the session?" you ask.

"I'll give it a go," says William. "I also propose we use timeboxing to help us stay focused."

Everyone nods in agreement. Ash volunteers to be timekeeper. William moves the first task into In Progress, and Ash dings the bell.

Do you:

- wait to see how the team gets on with the session on page 200, or
- leave the team to it on page 201?

## Hope Springs

You decide to remain with the team for a short while longer, just in case they need your assistance. You're confident that once the team gets going, they'll work together to achieve their goal.

You notice that William's relaxed and open style puts everyone at ease. What's more, his sense of humor helps unblock impasses during conversations and nudges people back on track.

In your experience, a successful engagement is one where you learn as much as you give. This has certainly been the case with the Dream Team. Your interaction with the team has shown you what a long way you've yet to go when it comes to applying agile values and principles not just at work, but outside of work too. You hope you'll have added enough value to their efforts by the end of your five days together.

You tell the team you'll be back at 11:30. It's time to prepare for this afternoon's presentation.

Continue with the adventure on page 201.

# Free Mind

In order to prepare yourself for some clear thinking, you decide to change your surroundings. You head over to the Rainbow Corridor to see if there's a place by the Green Team where you can sit quietly and think.

The Green Team space is empty when you arrive. According to their team calendar, they're at their midsprint review in meeting room 201.

You find an empty desk and look through the presentation notes you made last night.

Continue with the adventure on page 202.

## Begin with the End in Mind

Since reading *The Seven Habits of Highly Successful People* by Stephen R. Covey some years ago, you've developed a habit of always "beginning an endeavor with the end in mind." One example of this way of working is the user story you cowrote with Patrick at the start of this engagement.

You've learned that beginning with the end in mind (the goal) helps you stay focused when coming up with solutions (actions) and ensures you only do what's needed to achieve the goal (outcomes)—no more, no less (minimum effort for maximum value).

That's why you've chosen to use the picture of the future reality tree you created with Owen as the starting point for coming up with recommendations for the Dream Team.

If that future reality tree reflects accurately enough what Love Inc. wants to achieve as an organization, then your recommendations might not be relevant to just the Dream Team, but also to Love Inc. as a whole.

Continue with the adventure on page 203.

# Recommended Tools

You've identified six interrelated goals. You've also come up with a table of associated improvement actions to help the team, and the company, meet those goals. If applied correctly, the Dream Team may be able to work at a sustainable pace, be relatively stress-free, and deliver value now and in the foreseeable future.

| GOALS | TOOL | WHAT IT INVOLVES |
|---|---|---|
| Clear project goals | Business case | Defining clear goals |
| Clear project goals | Requirements definition of "done" | Defining clear goals and testable acceptance criteria for each story |
| Clear project goals | Product roadmap | Visualizing relationship between stories and how they fit into the bigger picture |
| Complementary requirements | Product ownership team | Product owners working as a team |
| Value-driven requirements | Business value estimates | Estimating user stories using relative business value or, ideally, a monetary currency |
| Clear scope | Business case | Ensuring everyone on the project understands what's in scope and what's not |
| Clear prioritization | Prioritization criteria | Ensuring everyone on the project knows what the criteria is and how to prioritize accordingly |
| Flow of work | Work-in-progress limit | Setting and refining WIP limit |

| GOALS | TOOL | WHAT IT INVOLVES |
|---|---|---|
| Flow of work | Process for dealing with blockers | Ensuring everyone on the project knows the process and adheres to it |
| Flow of work | Pull-based planning | Planning for what's achievable and creating options to pull into the current time box if team finishes early and agrees to do so |
| Flow of work | Daily stand-up | Team members sharing progress and blockers on a daily basis |
| Flow of work | Visual management | Visualizing progress with burndown and burnup charts, cumulative flow diagram |
| Flow of work | Timeboxing | Setting a fixed amount of time for working on a task—if the task isn't completed in that time, always start a new time box |

Continue with the adventure on page 205.

## Measure for Measure

In order to validate the improvement actions you've come up with, you look through the ones hanging off the Green Team's future reality tree poster. You find that there's a lot in common between the two sets of actions.

Next, you come up with a set of measures by which to gauge the team's performance improvement. To get an accurate view of the team's progress, the results of each measure must be considered as part of the same big picture, rather than looked at in isolation.

MEASURES

1. Clarity of goals measured by percentage of team members who understand the project goals (so the team knows what it's aiming for)

- Percentage of team members who understand the project goals (the higher the better)

2. Value measured by quantified business objectives (so that the team knows when it has released sufficient value to move on to the next project or when to choose to continue releasing value on the current one)

- Quantified business objectives based on the project's definition of value (to ensure requirements deliver the value identified for the project) as described in the article "Measurable Value with Agile" by Ryan Shriver

3. Quality measured by defects (so that the team knows how good its software is)

- Number of defects in production (this should decrease over time)

- Cycle time for resolving defects (this should decrease over time)

4. Flow measured by blocked items (so that the team can see the impact of blockers on flow)

- Number of blockers

- Cycle time for unblocking blockers

5. Flow measured by work items (so that the team focuses and stays focused on moving items from To Do into Done)

- Number of work items in progress (the fewer the better while making the most effective use of the team)

- Throughput of items from To Do to Done

- Other measures include cycle time and lead time—which measures you choose depend on what you're trying to optimize

6. Flow measured by team velocity (so that the team knows how effective its planning is)

- Number of stories planned vs. number of stories done per sprint

- Number of stories planned vs. number of stories done per release

It's almost a quarter past eleven. You know that Owen and the team will be returning from their midsprint review any minute now. You also remember that you've promised to return to the Dream Team to see how everyone got on with this morning's planning session.

Do you:

- ask Owen for feedback on your list on page 207, or
- head back to see the Dream Team on page 214?

## Troubled Waters

Owen and the Green Team are surprised to see you in their team space.

"Nice of you to visit," says Owen. "How can we help?"

You ask Owen if he has a few minutes to look over your recommendations for the Dream Team and the proposed measures to gauge team improvement in performance.

"Sure," says Owen. Owen mentions that their midsprint review hasn't gone well. Their product owner has started to use emotional blackmail to motivate the team.

"It's not like we're lazy and deliberately underachieving," says Owen. "Don't they know we're trying our best?"

You make a mental note of Owen's comments to discuss another time.

Continue with the adventure on page 208.

## Clear Goals

You know that the highest value task you can be doing right now is to get Owen's feedback on your work. Changing the way the Dream Team works is likely to have a positive impact on the way product ownership is implemented at Love Inc., and that in turn may help Owen and his team in the long term.

Owen is impressed by your improvement suggestions. He says, "If we only managed to clarify the project goals, we'd reduce the amount of noise and wasteful debates on why IT keeps delivering software that no one wants."

Owen adds that it's useful to see such a concrete list of suggestions from an expert like yourself. He says, "It's funny, but I wonder if the management team would pay as much attention if we made the same suggestions internally?"

You nod and explain that this is a common frustration among the staff members of organizations you work with. You consider it your responsibility as a consultant to voice the views and experiences of the people doing the work every day.

"Look at the time!" says Owen. "Let's walk and talk. I don't want to be late for our catch-up with the Dream Team."

Continue with the adventure on page 209.

## Moving Forward

On your way over to the Dream Team, Owen mentions that Ben popped by earlier and asked him to help review the latest options at 11:30.

By the time you and Owen reach the team space, you notice that not everyone is present.

"We're on a ten-minute break," Ben tells you. "Everyone will be back at 11:30 sharpish, as planned."

You wander around to find out firsthand how the session has gone.

"I feel absolutely exhausted," says Matt, "but it's been worth it. We've now got a list of delivery options prioritized iteratively: first by value and then by return on investment, dependencies, constraints, and risks."

Continue with the adventure on page 210.

## Shifting Sands

It's 11:30 and everyone's back.

Ash starts by summarizing the outcome of the session. It turns out that further details about certain requirements emerged during the discussions. That's why some of the effort estimates have gone up, while others have gone down.

OPTION 1—Full Online Self-Service

- BV: 150k, Cost: 240 story points, ROI: 625

- Includes: Arranging meetups, automated meetup reminders by text and email, posting feedback, and selective publishing of feedback

OPTION 2—Partial Online Self-Service with Improved User Tracking

- BV: 50k, Cost: 40 story points, ROI: 1250

- Includes: Arranging meetups only, plus basic web interface for operators to record operator-to-customer interactions

OPTION 3—Enhanced Customer Profiling and Recommendations

- BV: 70k, Cost: 45 story points, ROI: ???

- Includes: Enhanced customer profile by linking with LinkedIn, Twitter, and Facebook profiles, plus instant customer recommendations sent to customer

OPTION 4—Options 2 + 3

- BV: 120k, Cost: 85 story points, ROI: 1411

- Includes: Partial online self-service with improved user tracking and enhanced customer profiling and recommendations

OPTION 5—Option 2 + Part of Option 1

- BV: 90k, Cost: 105 story points, ROI: 857

- Includes: Partial online self-service with improved user tracking and arranging meetups only

OPTION 6—Option 3 + Part of Option 1

- BV: 110k, Cost: 110 story points, ROI: 1000

- Includes: Partial online self-service with improved user tracking and arranging meetups only

Continue with the adventure on page 212.

# Team Performance

Ash then asks for someone else from the team to continue with the summary. Cassandra volunteers.

"Based on the return on investment of the options as well as the associated risks, we all agree that option 4 is our preferred option. However, since agile is about keeping options open until the last responsible moment, here's the short list of our recommendations in order of preference."

1. OPTION 4—Options 2 + 3

   • BV: 120k, Cost: 85 story points, ROI: 1411

2. OPTION 6—Option 3 + Part of Option 1

   • BV: 110k, Cost: 110 story points, ROI: 1000

3. OPTION 5—Option 2 + Part of Option 1

   • BV: 90k, Cost: 105 story points, ROI: 857

Aidan says, "Since option 4 is our preferred option, we can also confirm that the two bundles of work can be easily split across the two teams, with Team Predator implementing the features of option 2 and the Dream Team implementing the features of option 3."

Then it's William's turn. He says, "We also recommend having both teams colocated and for us to hold joint daily scrums to make sure we all know what's going on and to deal with any blockers as efficiently and effectively as possible. We've already asked about the empty team space next to the Dream Team. It turns out Team Predator can move in once we get approval from management. They could move in this afternoon so we're ready to start Monday morning."

"The truth is, we should have invited Team Predator to be our neighbors a long time ago," says Ben.

Aidan smiles and replies, "If Rickard were here, I'm sure he'd agree that Team Predator should have figured that out and moved ourselves over months ago."

Continue with the adventure on page 213.

## Seeing Is Believing

"Good job," you say to everyone. "Anyone hungry?"

A crowd begins to head over to the cafeteria, with Aidan leading the way. Cassandra catches your eye. She wants to have a word with you.

"Jim, I just wanted to thank you for helping us out," she says. "This morning's been a real eye-opener for me. I didn't realize that I was working with people who cared so much about our product. I'm sorry I won't be able to join the team for lunch today, but I do plan to sit with both teams a couple of days a week going forward. Seeing François in action this morning has shown me that a true product owner can also be a member of the team."

You shake hands with Cassandra and thank her for her time this morning.

"By the way, will you put this up in the team space with the rest of the profile cards?" says Cassandra.

"Sure! See you this afternoon at the meeting with the management team," you say.

Continue with the adventure on page 215.

## Turning Point

You decide to head back to the Dream Team. The team is your top priority and, out of respect, it's important you show up on time.

On your way there, you bump into Owen. He mentions that Ben popped by earlier and asked him to help review the latest options at 11:30.

By the time you and Owen reach the team space, you notice that not everyone is present.

"We're on a ten-minute break," Ben tells you. "Everyone will be back at 11:30 sharpish, as planned."

You take this opportunity to find out firsthand how the session has gone.

"I feel absolutely exhausted," says Matt, "but it's been worth it. We've now got a list of delivery options prioritized iteratively, first by value and then by return on investment, dependencies, constraints, and risks."

Continue with the adventure on page 210.

# Growing Agile

There's a good agile turnout at lunch today.

You're glad to see Roger, William, Ethan, and Jason sit among the rest of the diners.

"Large team lunches seem to be in fashion these days," says William.

"Even the cafeteria staff have stopped stressing out about us moving the tables together and then moving them back again when we're done," says Ash.

François jumps straight in. "Working with the team this morning gave me the idea to start a community of practice for product ownership. That way, we can meet regularly to exchange ideas on how to produce higher-value requirements for our teams to implement."

"What's a community of practice?" asks Ethan.

"It's a group of people who want to share knowledge and experience in their chosen profession," replies François.

"I'm happy to start one for development," says Matt.

"And I'll do the same for analysis," says Rebecca.

"And I'll cover QA," says Nancy.

"Do I have to be an analyst to go to the analysis CoP?" asks Ethan.

"I'd say the main goal is to share knowledge and skills, so people should be free to participate based on their interests," says François. Heads nod around the table.

"We could also speak to guys working in UX to see if they'd be interested in starting one," says William. "That way, we can really learn from each other and improve the flow of value through our value chain!"

Continue with the adventure on page 216.

## Final Preparation

You feel recharged after the team lunch. Since you've still got work to do for this afternoon's presentation, you get up to go earlier than usual.

You estimate that it will take you about forty-five minutes to finalize the material for the presentation. That will take you until 1:15 p.m. The meeting isn't until 2 p.m.

You have a couple of options. After you've finished preparing the material, you can choose to go into the meeting without further feedback from others, or you can get feedback from a few volunteers from the team and improve the material based on that feedback.

Do you:

- get on with your work entirely on your own on page 217, or
- ask for volunteers to review your recommendations on page 219?

## The Missing Piece

It's almost time for the presentation to the management team.

You're glad that Patrick has agreed to the Dream Team being present at the meeting. This decision marks the beginning of a more open and collaborative way of working between management and the team.

You're happy with the quality of material you've produced, yet your gut tells you something's missing. Although you had a quick review with Owen on the first draft of the material, it will be the first time the Dream Team will be seeing the material, along with the management team.

You begin to wonder how the team will respond to your presentation.

Continue with the adventure on page 218.

## Fail

The presentation begins with Ben giving an overview of the delivery options identified earlier this morning. Then it's your turn to present the improvement actions and measures.

During the meeting, Patrick asks you how you came up with the recommendations. He wants to know if they were identified in collaboration with the team.

You explain that due to the tight deadline, there wasn't time to co-create them with the team. You had, however, reviewed them briefly with Owen. As you say this, you notice a look of disappointment among the team members.

The meeting eventually comes to an end, and everyone agrees that your recommendations are a sensible way forward.

You find out a few months later that the Dream Team only managed to implement a few of the improvements before inertia set in once again. You can't help but wonder if the team would have been more committed to implementing the recommendations had you involved them more. Maybe it's time to question how well you walk the walk of agile when under pressure.

THE END

# Volunteers

Before heading off to prepare for the presentation, you ask for volunteers to help review your material later on this afternoon. Ben, Matt, Aidan, and Owen offer to help.

This request prompts the question of who does what during the presentation. A few of you take this opportunity to come up with the agenda for the session.

1. Jim: Scene setting—user story of engagement

2. Ben: Two or more delivery options outlined, each of which provides at least 50 percent of the original business case for the release

3. Jim: Two or more recommendations for improving team performance

4. Jim: Measures for gauging improvement in team performance

5. Jim: Facilitation of questions and answers; team and Jim answer as appropriate

6. Patrick and Cassandra: Wrap-up

It's now time for you to prepare for the presentation.

Continue with the adventure on page 220.

# Simplicity

One of the most valuable things you've learned from applying agile is the effectiveness of using simple tools such as pen and paper. Instead of creating a slide presentation of your recommendations and measures, you decide to use flip chart paper and sticky notes instead.

This approach not only makes presentations more interesting for the audience, but it also enables you to respond to any points raised by adapting your presentation in real time. What's more, the team can choose to reuse the posters and sticky notes to start planning and tracking which improvement actions to implement right away.

You can always capture the material as a slide presentation afterward if that's what people find useful.

Continue with the adventure on page 221.

# Future Reality

You begin by drawing a copy of the Green Team's future reality tree on a single sheet of flip chart paper. You then write down one improvement action/tool per shaded sticky note and place each one next to its corresponding goal. You also number the tools to indicate the logical sequence for applying the tools one at a time.

## *Future Reality Tree*

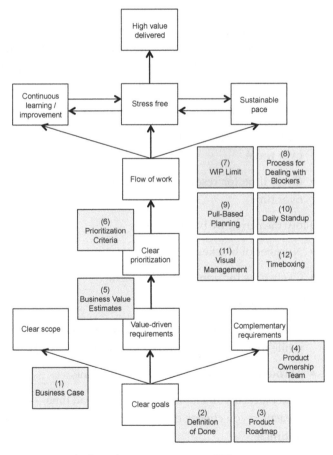

Continue with the adventure on page 258.

# Measurable Improvements

You create a third poster detailing the measures, or units of measurement, for gauging improvement in team performance.

MEASURES

1. Clarity of goals

   • Percentage of team members who understand the project goals (the higher the better)

2. Value

   • Quantified business objectives based on the project's definition of value (to ensure requirements deliver the value identified for the project) as described in the article "Measurable Value with Agile" by Ryan Shriver

3. Quality measured by defects

   • Number of defects in production (this should decrease over time)

   • Cycle time for resolving defects (this should decrease over time)

4. Flow measured by blocked items

   • Number of blockers

   • Cycle time for unblocking blockers

5. Flow measured by work items

   • Number of work items in progress (the fewer the better while making the most effective use of the team)

   • Throughput of items from To Do to Done

   • Other measures include cycle time and lead time—which measures you choose depend on what you're trying to optimize

6. Flow measured by team velocity

   • Number of stories planned vs. number of stories done per sprint

- Number of stories planned vs. number of stories done per release

IMPORTANT NOTE: To get an accurate view of the team's progress, the results of each measure must be considered as part of the same big picture, rather than looked at in isolation.

Continue with the adventure on page 224.

# The Perfection Game

It's time to get feedback from Ben, Matt, Aidan, and Owen on the material you've prepared.

To make the process of giving and receiving feedback effective, efficient, and fun, you suggest playing the Perfection Game as a group.

The Perfection Game consists of three questions to be answered by each person giving the feedback.

1.  What would you give the piece of work being reviewed out of 10? (where 10 is high and 1 is low)

2.  What do you like about the piece of work?

3.  What would make the piece of work perfect? (achieve 10/10)

You explain that, based on the principle of continuous improvement, perfection isn't something attainable but rather something you constantly strive for.

"That reminds me of a saying by the French poet Paul Valéry. 'A poem is never finished, only abandoned,'" says William.

"I've always thought of myself as a perfectionist, but agile is teaching me to be a value-driven craftsman instead," says Matt. "The ultimate goal isn't perfection, it's delivering quality software to meet the customer's needs."

Continue with the adventure on page 225.

# Group Smarts

You begin by giving a brief overview of the improvement actions and measures. Then you give everyone five minutes to play the Perfection Game.

Below is the combined feedback from Ben, Matt, Aidan, and Owen.

1. Score out of 10? 7/10–8/10

2. What do you like about the piece of work?

- Visual presentation makes it easier to follow

- Representation of the cause and effect of each improvement action

- Captures what we need to do on a single sheet of paper!

- Explanation of what each improvement action entails

- Jim attributes credit to the Green Team for the creation of the tree

- Improvement actions can be applied to the majority of the teams at Love Inc. to bring about systemic change

- Multiple measures are used to prevent people from gaming the system and skewing the actual outcome and benefits

3. What would make it perfect?

- Include technical recommendations

- Include a written explanation for each improvement action (perhaps on a separate sheet)

- Would have liked to involve the entire Dream Team in defining the measures

Continue with the adventure on page 226.

## Value Add

"Thanks for your ideas," you say.

You overhear Ethan say to William, "How does he make asking and receiving feedback look so easy?"

You reply, "I know that if we work together, we can come up with better ideas than I can on my own. More importantly, I like to think of feedback as a gift, so thank you."

"The gift of feedback? That's got to be a 'Jimism,'" says Matt with a chuckle.

You smile and continue. "Let's go through each of the improvement ideas. Regarding technical recommendations: Patrick and I have agreed to focus on process improvements for now. The plan is for the team to come up with technical improvements afterward. As for including a written explanation for each improvement action, that's a great suggestion. Anyone want to pair with me to write those up? We have thirty minutes before the meeting."

Ben and Matt want to go back to see how the team is doing. Owen volunteers.

"Thanks, Owen," you say. "Last but not least, the measures are intended to be suggestions based on my limited knowledge, skills, and experience. I strongly recommend the team holds a measures definition session next week to come up with its own list of possible measures to implement."

"And maybe we can make it a joint exercise with the Green Team so we can then make systemic improvements," suggests Ben.

"That's a great idea!" you say. "Thanks again everyone for all the feedback."

Continue with the adventure on page 227.

# Showdown

It's time to head over to the meeting room. You like to arrive ten minutes early to give yourself plenty of time to set up. You're not surprised to find that Nancy, Rebecca, and Ash are already in the room.

"Just let us know if you need anything," says Rebecca.

"Always happy to help," adds Ash.

You sense that everyone's feeling at once nervous and excited, including you. The feeling in the room reminds you of Nancy's quote about drama being defined as a combination of anticipation and uncertainty.

Within minutes, Patrick arrives with Cassandra and Cassandra's boss, Hugh, the head of marketing. They're followed by the rest of the management team.

Continue with the adventure on page 228.

## Revitalized

You begin by welcoming everyone and setting the scene for the meeting. You then construct a kanban board complete with sticky note tasks.

The meeting backlog looks like this:

- Scene setting — Jim
- Delivery options — Ben + team
- Recommendations for improving team performance — Jim
- Measures for gauging improvement in team performance — Jim
- Questions and answers: Jim + all
- Session wrap-up: Patrick and Cassandra

The hour-long meeting goes by in a flash. Everyone is visibly engaged, building on each other's points as well as raising risks and concerns about what lies ahead. You have never seen so many people at Love Inc. looking so animated outside of lunchtime.

Continue with the adventure on page 229.

# All's Well That Ends Well

The time has come for Patrick and Cassandra to wrap up the meeting.

Patrick begins. "First of all, Cassandra and I want to thank both the team and Jim for all their hard work and dedication this week. We also want to extend our thanks to Team Predator and the Green Team for their help. Last, but not least, we want to thank the management team for their continued support."

"Speaking on behalf of the management team, it has come to our attention that some things need to change. For instance, we need stop incentives that create conflict instead of collaboration. Going forward, we'd like to hear your ideas on how we can improve the way the company's run."

Then it's over to Cassandra. "Regarding this project, it's clear that we have a long road ahead of us. From a personal perspective, I know it won't be easy, but if this week's progress is anything to go by, then the next six weeks is sure to be one heck of a roller coaster ride."

By the end of the meeting, everyone agrees to reconvene first thing Monday morning to choose a delivery option, as well as to include some of the improvement actions you have suggested into their plan.

"We are also hoping that Jim will stay and help ensure we deliver the release," adds Cassandra as she turns to you with a smile.

Two things are for certain. One, you know you've had a positive influence on the Dream Team. Two, you are very much looking forward to continuing this adventure with the team. Your journey toward change that endures has only just begun.

THE END

## LOVE INC. COMPANY REVIEW: THE COMPANY AND THE CONCEPT

Love Inc. began two and a half years ago as a start-up with limited seed money. It hired a number of talented people with lots of great ideas. Within a year, it launched an online dating experience where people could find and connect with one another in a safe and secure online forum. Since its launch a year and a half ago, it's won a number of awards, including Best User Experience. Love Inc.'s continued success is reflected by its steady and ever-increasing revenue and growth.

Although there were already a number of successful online dating start-ups, the services they offered were limited. Many of the websites resembled job sites, with only basic profile and search functionality. Some people found this approach off-putting, particularly high-net-worth professionals with neither the time nor the inclination for what seemed like a gamble for something as serious as finding a lifelong relationship. This group was to become the target market for Love Inc.'s flagship application, called Happily Ever After.

## MODUS OPERANDI

Love Inc. believes in shared value through shared values. Its seven values are communication, simplicity, feedback, courage, respect, trust, and integrity. These values are intended not only for its employees but for their customer community too.

## TRUE LOVE WITH A MONEY-BACK GUARANTEE

Love Inc. takes pride in being the first and only company to offer a money-back dating guarantee based on a "shared value, shared risk" model. This helps ensure that both customers and the company benefit from doing business together. The business model became so famous that even those who knew little about online dating came to know Love Inc. as "the fairest of them all."

## COMPANY CHALLENGES

Being best in class comes with its own set of challenges. The second phase of Project Happily Ever After began six months ago. A core group of business representatives got together to come up with the next big idea. Within days, they had two hundred ideas and found themselves mired in unnecessary detail. Since then, they've attempted to turn ideas from concept to cash on countless occasions but with little success.

## ANALYSIS PARALYSIS

As the business struggled to think outside the box and evaluate its ideas, it found itself constrained by what seemed like excessive cost for making the most trivial of changes to the existing product. It became clear, though difficult to accept, that this technical debt was partly due to corners that had been cut to meet the deadline of the product's initial launch.

## BUSINESS VS. IT

Although the business managers and the IT staff had forged a strong sense of camaraderie as a result of the long hours they spent working together to get the product launched, they now find themselves in a deadlock fueled by mistrust, discontent, and low morale.

## WHERE HAS ALL THE LOVE GONE?

As Love Inc. finds itself embroiled in internal turmoil, the vision that everyone can live happily ever after seems but a dim and distant dream, one that's threatening to tear the company apart.

Do you:

- review the email describing the goals of your mission at Love Inc. on page 242, or
- continue with the adventure on page 5?

## Know It All

You call a team meeting and explain the desperate challenge that lies before them.

"We know all about continuous improvement, thank you very much," says Jason. "When it comes to agile, we've been there, done that, bought the T-shirt."

You push on and describe the improvement plan the team needs to implement right away based on your past knowledge and experience in dealing with such situations.

"Isn't agile all about 'individuals and interactions over processes and tools'?" quips Roger. "It sounds like you're trying to tell us what to do, just like the managers. What happened to self-organizing teams?"

The tension in the room is thick enough to cut with a knife.

Rebecca, a business analyst says, "Jim, we understand where you're coming from, but we aren't like the other teams you've worked with. We are different. We have a certain way of getting things done around here."

You sense Rebecca is only trying to help, but you've heard it all before. It seems the team is resisting change by coming up with excuses. Desperate times require desperate measures. Doesn't the team realize you're only trying to help?

Your face feels warm, and your fist hits the table. "These are all excuses I've heard before," you say. "The challenges you face are by no means unique. The fact is, organizations are made up of people. Consequently, the problems they face are similar—often the same. The key differentiating factor is scale. I've worked in plenty of organizations much larger and more complex than this one."

Jason looks you straight in the eye and says, "Who died and put you in charge?"

Both Jason and Roger are now standing with their arms crossed, while others remain firmly wedged in their seats, staring either at the floor or at the door. You recognize all the signs of fight and flight around the room.

You quickly draw the meeting to a close and explain that you'll organize a follow-up meeting to discuss next steps for first thing tomorrow.

After lunch, you get a call from Patrick, the manager who hired you. He wants to see you in his office right away.

Continue with the adventure on page 6.

## Coach's Log: Day 1

February 1

ACTIVITIES

- Had one-on-one conversations with all team members (excluding the product owner)

- Scheduled project retrospective for tomorrow

- Walked about on my own during lunch

- Got project scope and requirements overview from Rebecca

- Got technical design and implementation walk-through from Ash and Roger

WHAT WENT WELL

- Got to know the team members through one-on-one conversations

WHAT WENT WRONG

- Haven't met product owner yet

PUZZLES

- How quickly can I arrange to speak to the product owner?

IMPROVEMENT ACTIONS

- Ask team members for more real-time input and feedback so that I can serve them better.

DAY RATING: 7/10

Continue with the adventure on page 29.

# Coach's Log: Day 1

February 1

ACTIVITIES

- Had one-on-one conversations with all team members (excluding the product owner)

- Scheduled project retrospective for tomorrow

- Went for personal walk during lunch

- Got project scope and requirements overview from Rebecca

- Got technical design and implementation walk-through from Ash and Roger

- Discovered Team Predator's team space

WHAT WENT WELL

- Got to know the team members through one-on-one conversations

- Identified potential new friends: Team Predator

WHAT WENT WRONG

- Haven't met product owner yet

PUZZLES

- How quickly can I arrange to speak to the product owner?

IMPROVEMENT ACTIONS

- Ask team members for more real-time input and feedback so that I can serve them better.

DAY RATING: 8/10

Continue with the adventure on page 29.

## Your Mission

*To:* Patrick Dearlove <p.dearlove@loveinc.com>

*From:* Jim Hopper <jimhopper@jimhopper.com>

*Subject:* Coaching Goals for the Dream Team

*Date:* January 3

Hi Patrick,

Many thanks for your time last week. Below are the agreed-upon goals and the acceptance criteria for my five-day engagement in the format of a user story based on our conversation.

I look forward to meeting the team in person.

Many thanks,

Jim

PROVIDE RECOMMENDATIONS

As a management team, we need a list of recommendations so that the Dream Team delivers some value for this release and knows how to improve its team performance over time.

ACCEPTANCE CRITERIA

- Two or more delivery options outlined, each of which provides at least 50 percent of the original business case for the release

- Two or more recommendations for improving team performance

- Measures for gauging improvement in team performance

Do you:

- continue with the adventure on page 5, or
- first review a confidential company report compiled by an external consultancy on page 230?

# Lighten Up

The room feels stuffy. A few people look moody. You decide to run the profile card exercise to dispel the tension in the room.

"Everyone take an index card and a couple of markers," you say. "To help us get to know each other better, write down your name, a pet love, and a pet hate on your index card," you continue. "Last, but not least, include a portrait of yourself. The success criteria for the portrait is that we should be able to recognize you in the corridor from the drawing. You have three minutes. Ready, steady, go!" You ding the bell and people jump into action.

Roger lets out a loud sigh and says, "I can't draw to save my life!"

"What a waste of time," Jason mutters.

"Consider this a test of whether or not you know each other as well as you think," you reply. "You have just under three minutes remaining."

William glances over Rebecca's shoulder and chuckles. Rebecca sticks her tongue out at William and embellishes her index card with extra art. Suppressed laughter ripples through the room.

You ding the bell. "Time's up. You now have two minutes to introduce yourself to as many team members as possible using your index card," you say. "Ready, steady, go." You ding the bell once again.

Nancy and Ben leap out of their seats, followed by everyone else. The room is now filled with giggles as people exchange mutual looks of embarrassment.

You ding the bell again. People return to their seats with a spring in their step. The mood in the room has been lifted, as you had anticipated.

Jason coughs to clear his throat. "Exactly what was the purpose of that exercise?" he asks.

"What do you think?" you ask everyone.

"It proves that we barely know each other at all and yet we claim to be a team," says William. "It's no wonder we're in such a mess."

"And to remind us that we used to enjoy working with each other," adds Ben.

"To be honest, I now understand you all a bit better," says Nancy. "For instance, I never knew Roger felt so strongly about laziness. It explains why he gets moody when we cut corners because something's difficult to do."

"With everyone's permission, we'll stick the cards up in the team space to liven up the area and attract visitors. Meanwhile, let's stick them up over there on the wall."

You walk over and stick up your profile card. As the cards appear on the wall, everyone starts chatting again.

"I like your ride," says Matt to William, pointing at the picture of a purple camper van.

"It's the same color as the one I had in college," replies William. "Only this one's fitted with all the modcons you can imagine!"

"Maybe when we get to know each other better, we can go on a team road trip to the annual Star Trek conference," suggests Rebecca.

"Actually, I'm a bit of Trekkie, too," says Ethan. Jason smiles with a look of surprise.

Continue with the adventure on page 239.

## The Profile Card Exercise

Continue with the adventure on page 42.

## Busted

You've heard enough. You are shocked by the false accounts of what happened. You feel angry at the team's betrayal.

"It's all lies," you blurt out. "Jason's never going to be on board with my techniques, and it seems that Roger has decided to join him. Can't you see they're sabotaging my attempt to make things better?"

To make matters worse, you blame Jason for low team morale and code quality. "It's time Jason is removed from the team," you say.

Patrick looks you straight in the eye and says, "Thank you for your help, Jim. It's best we continue the project without you."

Patrick asks his secretary to escort you out of the office. Before you know it, you're back on the street.

It feels like you've been punched in the gut. Thoughts swirl in your head. Should have. Would have. Could have. You decide to take time out to reflect on what's happened. You're not quite ready to give up doing a job you love. Not yet.

THE END

## Your Mission

*To:* Patrick Dearlove <p.dearlove@loveinc.com>

*From:* Jim Hopper <jimhopper@jimhopper.com>

*Subject:* Coaching Goals for the Dream Team

*Date:* January 3

Hi Patrick,

Many thanks for your time last week. Below are the agreed-upon goals and the acceptance criteria for my five-day engagement in the format of a user story based on our conversation.

I look forward to meeting the team in person.

Many thanks,

Jim

PROVIDE RECOMMENDATIONS

As a management team, we need a list of recommendations so that the Dream Team delivers some value for this release and knows how to improve its team performance over time.

ACCEPTANCE CRITERIA

- Two or more delivery options outlined, each of which provides at least 50 percent of the original business case for the release

- Two or more recommendations for improving team performance

- Measures for gauging improvement in team performance

Continue with the adventure on page 5.

# Eat, Play, Work

At noon, you make your way over to the cafeteria.

You nod and smile as you sit down with your tray of lasagna and garlic bread. Nothing like a filling lunch for the demanding afternoon ahead.

The whole of the Dream Team sits around two tables deliberately put together.

"Looks like a full house today," you say. "What's the special occasion?"

"It's good to have rest days when you're training hard," says Roger, with a serious look on his face, while the rest of the team laughs.

"It's been a long week, and I'm not sick of the sight of you all yet!" says William with a smile as he waves a fist at everyone.

Continue with the adventure on page 175.

# More Team One-on-Ones

In the afternoon, you continue with the series of conversations with the other four team members. It seems everyone has a similar story to tell. At the end of your conversation with Ethan, he asks the question everyone else is wondering about.

"Do you think you can help us turn things around?" he says.

"Many things become possible when people choose to work together," you say.

The series of one-on-ones have been intense and invaluable. You want to speak to Cassandra, the product owner, as soon as possible, but you discover she's away on business and won't be back until next week.

Continue with the adventure on page 245.

# Information Gathering

Later on in the afternoon, after you've spoken individually with the nine available team members, you offer them each a cookie to go with their coffee.

Meanwhile, you ask people about their availability for a team meeting, a project retrospective. You explain that the meeting is a chance for everyone to share their thoughts about where the project is at and how to move it forward together.

You schedule the meeting for tomorrow afternoon from 2 to 4 p.m., because that's when everyone's available.

Next, you need to find out about the software product the team is building. Everyone seems very busy, so you ask for volunteers to get you up to speed.

You spend the first half of the afternoon with Rebecca, who talks you through the project scope and gives you a status update on the requirements implemented and those yet to be implemented.

After that, Ash and Roger jointly walk you through the design and implementation details.

Continue with the adventure on page 246.

## Trouble

According to Ash and Roger, some of the brand-new software components already require reengineering from scratch. You're reminded once again how a piece of software can tell you a lot about the team that built it. Judging by the way the software is rotting from the inside out, the Dream Team is dysfunctional at best.

In order to find out more about the project, you pose the following questions to Rebecca, Ash, and Roger.

Continue with the adventure on page 247.

## Project Evaluation

The questions are divided into four categories: value, cost, quality, and time. You write down the responses next to each question.

VALUE

- *Question: How is business value calculated and measured?*

  Answer: No idea.

- *Question: How accurate is estimated business value compared with actual value delivered by the project?*

  Answer: No idea.

COST

- *Question: How is effort calculated and measured?*

  Answer: Using story points—the number of points per sprint-level story is determined by the amount of effort required to deliver the story and by the complexity of the story.

- *Question: How accurate is estimated effort compared with actual effort delivered per release?*

  Answer: Very inaccurate.

- *Question: How much does it cost the business to make a release?*

  Answer: A lot; after development ends, there's a four-week regression testing period

- *Question: How much per release do defects cost the business (such as loss of new business but not including cost of remediation)?*

  Answer: We don't track that, although we probably should, now that you mention it.

QUALITY

- *Question: How many defects are there per release?*

  Answer: Less than a hundred?

- *Question: What is the cost of remediation per release?*

  Answer: Probably as much as the cost of feature development.

- *Question: How long does it take to discover a defect?*

  Answer: Depends, sometimes a week, sometimes as long as a month.

TIME

- *Question: How long does it take for a requirement to get from an idea to the end customer?*

  Answer: Quickest is eight weeks; it usually takes longer.

- *Question: How long does it take for a requirement to get from being planned to the end customer?*

  Answer: Quickest has been five weeks, but those were exceptions. In general, it takes one to two months.

- *How often is software released? When was the last release? And the release previous to that one?*

  Answer: Can't remember the last time we released; must be over three months ago.

Continue with the adventure on page 249.

## Relief

The key to information gathering is consistent questioning and an open mind. A common complaint among the team members is that requirements that have little to do with the project are always given top priority.

To ensure you get a balanced view, you plan to pose the same questions to Cassandra, the product owner, when she becomes available.

It's been a fruitful first day. It's almost time to go home.

Do you:

- write your daily log on page 234 or
- go for a walk to help you reflect on the day on page 250?

# Walkabout

You like to explore the physical space where you work. The layout of an office, along with its furniture, can tell you as much about a company's culture as the people do.

Hidden from the usual flow of human traffic, behind a wall, is a team space covered in sticky notes. Like the Dream Team's space, each desk has a pair of monitors. However, instead of one keyboard and mouse per computer, there are two. This is a sign that the team does pair programming.

On the wall is a poster of a Predator, the creature from the film of the same name. Beside it is a group picture annotated with each team member's name and phone number.

In the middle of the wall is the team's kanban board, with a work-in-progress limit of three in the In Progress column. According to the team's burndown chart, the team is halfway through sprint 2 of their next release.

Although the team's current velocity is slightly lower than its linear burndown rate, the team has stuck to its WIP limit of three. Of the three WIP items, one is blocked by two impediments: one dated a week ago and another dated today. Someone called Aidan is responsible for taking care of both impediments.

These bits of information give you the impression of a healthy and performant team. You plan to introduce yourself to Team Predator sometime. For now, you find a quiet corner to reflect on Day 1 before heading home.

Continue with the adventure on page 235.

## Review Your Mission

Before returning to the team space, you take time out to remind yourself of the goals of the engagement. It's important to always have the end in mind if you're to achieve your goals.

During your first meeting with Patrick, you cowrote the goals along with the acceptance criteria in the form of a user story. Below is what you both agreed on up front. Patrick made it clear back then that, given the recent poor delivery record of the team, delivery is now top priority, followed by ideas for helping the team improve its process.

PROVIDE RECOMMENDATIONS

As a management team, we need a list of recommendations so that the Dream Team delivers some value for this release and knows how to improve its team performance over time.

ACCEPTANCE CRITERIA

- Two or more delivery options outlined, each of which provide at least 50 percent of the original business case for the release

- Two or more recommendations for improving team performance

- Measures for gauging improvement in team performance

During that conversation, Patrick had reassured you that the project backlog contains items of significant business value. When you had asked about how the business value has been calculated and tracked to date, Patrick had explained that it's been difficult for the business to quantify the estimated value of the business proposition. He'd like to hear your ideas on how to do this at some point.

Continue with the adventure on page 252.

## Look Ahead

You take a moment to verify your progress in relation to your plan for the rest of the week. Since yesterday you've been assessing the team's current performance through informal discussions with team members. This afternoon's project retrospective should provide more information on the challenges and obstacles that the team faces.

On Wednesday morning, you plan to baseline the project's current state. On Wednesday afternoon, you'll facilitate a planning session between the team and the product owner to come up with a short list of delivery options.

This potentially leaves you Thursday and Friday morning to do your recommendations report. Since the report will take between half a day to a day to prepare, there's some slack built into your schedule. You suspect you'll need it.

It's time to get Day 2 started with the team.

Continue with the adventure on page 36.

## Review Your Mission

Before returning to the team space, you take time out to remind yourself of the goals of the engagement. It's important to always have the end in mind if you're to achieve your goals.

During your first meeting with Patrick, you cowrote the goals along with the acceptance criteria in the form of a user story. Below is what you both agreed on up front. Patrick made it clear back then that, given the recent poor delivery record of the team, delivery is now top priority, followed by ideas for helping the team improve its process.

PROVIDE RECOMMENDATIONS

As a management team, we need a list of recommendations so that the Dream Team delivers some value for this release and knows how to improve its team performance over time.

ACCEPTANCE CRITERIA

- Two or more delivery options outlined, each of which provide at least 50 percent of the original business case for the release

- Two or more recommendations for improving team performance

- Measures for gauging improvement in team performance

During that conversation, Patrick had reassured you that the project backlog contains items of significant business value. When you had asked about how the business value has been calculated and tracked to date, Patrick had explained that it's been difficult for the business to quantify the estimated value of the business proposition. He'd like to hear your ideas on how to do this at some point.

Continue with the adventure on page 254.

## Look Ahead

You take a moment to verify your progress in relation to your plan for the rest of the week. Since yesterday you've been assessing the team's current performance through informal discussions with team members. This afternoon's project retrospective should provide more information on the challenges and obstacles that the team faces.

On Wednesday morning, you plan to baseline the project's current state. On Wednesday afternoon, you'll facilitate a planning session between the team and the product owner to come up with a short list of delivery options.

This potentially leaves you Thursday and Friday morning to do your recommendations report. Since the report will take between half a day to a day to prepare, there's some slack built into your schedule. You suspect you'll need it.

It's time to get Day 2 started with the team.

Continue with the adventure on page 255.

# Uninvited Guest

You ask everyone to gather around for a quick update on today's planned activities. To test the waters, you mention that there's a possibility that Patrick will be present at the project retrospective.

"I don't think that's a good idea," says Nancy.

"I thought you were here to help us," says Roger quietly.

"What doesn't make it a good idea?" you ask.

Matt, the former Scrum master, looks around the room and then says, "The management fixes the deadline and the budget but then allows the business to keep increasing the scope. At the rate we're going, we'll never finish the project."

Given the team's response, you decide to ask Patrick not to attend the meeting. You remind everyone to reconvene in the afternoon for the project retrospective and thank them for their time.

Continue with the adventure on page 38.

# True Agile

Team Predator is adamant that "they're no experts" when it comes to agile. Instead of "doing agile" or "being agile," the team refers to what it does as "learning agile."

"Agile's a journey that never ends," says Aidan, "at least according to those who don't just talk the talk but walk the walk." He strikes his chest with his fist as he says this to show his sincerity.

Everyone laughs, including you.

"We're in it for the long run!" says Barry, a tester wearing a T-shirt that says "I don't have to be superhero to do great things." "Even though we call our two-week time boxes sprints, it's more like running a marathon. That's why we try to work at a sustainable pace."

"It can be tough at times, though," says Rickard, "so we remind each other by saying, 'Show me the money!' We're referring to the business value of the requirements, of course, to ensure we don't waste unnecessary time on low value and costly items that aren't really needed."

"Absolutely!" says François, their product owner from Dijon. François tells you how he went from sitting on the third floor full-time to sitting with the team on the first floor for two days a week shortly after the project began. He describes learning agile as requiring serious dedication. "It's also good for the heart," he says as he gives Annabel a wink.

The walk has done you good. You're glad to have discovered such friendly neighbors. You feel recharged and are ready for the challenge ahead. You thank everybody on Team Predator for their time and their stories.

As Rickard walks you out he tells you, "We're always learning about how to apply agile better. Maybe we can meet up sometime to exchange ideas?"

You say that, if everything goes well this week, your contract may be extended and you two can catch up next week when you'll have more time.

As you leave, Aidan calls out, "Come back and visit us whenever you need to!"

You turn to wave and smile.

Continue with the adventure on page 92.

# Recommended Tools

You create a second poster containing the table of associated improvement actions to help the team, and the company, meet the goals in the future reality tree.

| GOALS | TOOL | WHAT IT INVOLVES |
|---|---|---|
| Clear project goals | Business case | Defining clear goals |
| Clear project goals | Requirements definition of "done" | Defining clear goals and testable acceptance criteria for each story |
| Clear project goals | Product roadmap | Visualizing relationship between stories and how they fit into the bigger picture |
| Complementary requirements | Product owner-ship team | Product owners working as a team |
| Value-driven requirements | Business value estimates | Estimating user stories using relative business value or, ideally, a monetary currency |
| Clear scope | Business case | Ensuring everyone on the project understands what's in scope and what's not |
| Clear prioritiza-tion | Prioritization Criteria | Ensuring everyone on the project knows what the criteria is and how to prioritize accordingly |
| Flow of work | Work-in-progress limit | Setting and refining WIP limit |
| Flow of work | Process for dealing with blockers | Ensuring everyone on the project knows the process and adheres to it |
| Flow of work | Pull-based planning | Planning for what's achievable and creating |

| GOALS | TOOL | WHAT IT INVOLVES |
|---|---|---|
| | | options to pull into the current time box if team finishes early and agrees to do so |
| Flow of work | Daily stand-up | Team members sharing progress and blockers on a daily basis |
| Flow of work | Visual management | Visualizing progress with burndown and burnup charts, cumulative flow diagram |
| Flow of work | Timeboxing | Setting a fixed amount of time for working on a task—if the task isn't completed in that time, always start a new time box |

These two posters—the recommended tools and the future reality tree—together contain your recommendations for improving the Dream Team's team performance.

Continue with the adventure on page 222.

# Part II

# Appendices

APPENDIX 1

# Who's Who

INDIVIDUALS

- Jim—you, the agile coach
- Emily—your girlfriend
- Patrick—head of IT at Love Inc.

THE DREAM TEAM

- Cassandra—product owner
- Rebecca—business analyst
- Nancy—tester
- Jason—developer
- Matt—developer
- Roger—developer
- Ben—developer
- Ash—developer
- William—developer
- Ethan—developer

TEAM PREDATOR

- François—product owner
- Rickard—Scrum master
- Annabel—business analyst
- Barry—tester

- Aidan—developer
- Seth—developer
- Danny—developer
- Wendy—developer

THE GREEN TEAM

- Owen—Scrum master
- Brian—developer
- Rest of team...

# LinkedIn: Jim Hopper

Agile consultant-coach with a passion for people, process, and continuous improvement, in search of projects and teams that want to challenge themselves to do better. Assists teams in delivering more business value faster for less cost. Specializes in the pragmatic application of agile methods and lean.

EXPERIENCE

Hopper Consulting—Agile Consultant-Coach

- The Big Cookie Company: Coached one team as part of a pilot project to try agile

- Griffiths & Bond Private Banking: Created and delivered intermediate agile training to teams with 5+ years of agile; trained trainers to deliver training, as well as coached 6 individual delivery teams (3 in UK, 1 in US, 1 in APAC)

- Skymiles: Coached 2 teams as part of a company-wide initiative to adopt agile

- World Airlines: Coached 3 teams as part of a company-wide initiative to adopt agile

Independent Broadcasting Corporation

- Development Manager: Introduced Scrum into the IT department as part of a continuous improvement initiative

*Money Matters*: The Financial Journal

- Software Developer: Delivered Java-based projects as full-time Java developer using a combination of waterfall, PRINCE2, and extreme programming (XP)

SKILLS AND EXPERTISE

- Agile methodologies (specializing in Scrum, XP, Kanban, and lean software development), project management, requirements analysis, software development, organizational change, teaching, coaching, facilitation, public speaking, systems thinking

EDUCATION

- B.S. in computer science: Northwestern University, Chicago

RECOMMENDATIONS

- "Jim is one of the most inspiring people I've met professionally. Jim brings out the best in people. It will be difficult to continue our agile journey without him." — Monica Randall, agile transformation lead, The Big Cookie Company

- "Jim joined us at a time when agile was 'working' and was starting to become viral in the organization. Jim was the perfect choice for taking the agile transformation to the next level." — Andrew Lebowski, director, Griffiths & Bond Private Banking

- "Jim's technical background and focus on delivering value has helped motivate the developers to think like the business. His ability to nurture team spirit has brought IT and the business closer together so that we work as one team." — Robert Watson, developer, Griffiths & Bond Private Banking

- "Jim is one of the most energetic agile coaches I've come across. He's a people person and is 100 percent focused on doing his best. Jim's constantly on the lookout to help an organization improve by improving himself." — Noah Greenspan, team lead, Skymiles

- "Jim is a fantastic coach, leader, and presenter. He explains complex concepts in a way that makes learning fun and practical. It has been a pleasure learning from and working with Jim."—Jessica Donaldson, project manager, World Airlines

- "Jim challenges the status quo and strives to achieve true, lasting cultural change within an organization."—Bill Richardson, head of IT and architecture, Independent Broadcasting Corporation

Return to the adventure on page 2.

APPENDIX 3

# Glossary

Key terms, concepts, and topics found in the story are defined here. For more details, I suggest looking at *Bedtime Reading*.

*acceptance criteria*   A set of testable criteria that confirms when the goal of a work item has been achieved; usually related to a product backlog item

*agile (aka agile methods)*   An increasingly popular way of managing software development and projects; describes a way of working that is iterative, incremental, value-driven, collaborative, and customer-focused; originated as a set of values and principles on which the family of agile methods such as Scrum, Kanban, XP (extreme programming) and DSDM are based; see also *agile values and principles*

*agile coach*   A coach who is knowledgeable on the subject of agile and has practical experience; likely to have worked on one or more agile projects in a number of companies with varying degrees of success; typically responsible for leading and coaching an organization in using agile

*agile values and principles*   The set of four values and twelve principles defined in the Agile Manifesto[1]

*backlog*   A collection of work items, such as user stories, that can be used to represent a project's scope; also known as *product backlog* in Scrum

---

1.   www.agilemanifesto.org

*blocker (aka impediment)*  Something that prevents someone from making immediate progress

*burndown chart*  A chart with a downward trend; usually short for *sprint burndown chart* in Scrum, a chart that tracks the total number of stories to be completed, or "burned down," in a sprint, decrementing over time by the number of stories completed—an alternative to burning down by stories is to burn down by story points

*burnup chart*  A chart with an upward trend; usually short for *value burnup chart*, a chart that goes from zero business value delivered to an increase in business value delivered over time ("burned up") such as a sprint or release; see also *business value*

*business value*  Represents the value delivered by a piece of work; ideally measured in a monetary currency (such as a dollar amount); more commonly expressed in terms of relative business value points between work items to facilitate prioritization where a monetary value is not available; see *business value point*

*business value point*  The unit in which the value generated by a piece of work is estimated; see also *business value, relative estimation,* and *T-shirt sizing*

*cause-effect diagram*  A problem-solving tool that visualizes factors in terms of causes and their effects on a process or system

*community of practice (CoP)*  A group of people who want to share knowledge and experience in their chosen profession

*cumulative flow diagram (CFD)*  A chart that tracks progress by showing the amount of average work in progress and the average cycle time of a user story through different phases in a delivery cycle, such as identification through to analysis, development, testing, and release —in agile, these phases are typically concurrent activities in practice

*current reality tree*   A tool for identifying root causes to problems in a system; one of the thinking processes in the Theory of Constraints

*daily scrum (aka daily stand-up)*   A fifteen-minute meeting at which team members stay standing while synchronizing the work for the team for the next twenty-four hours; each person answers the following three questions: What did I do yesterday? What will I do today? Any blockers, and if so, what are they?

*DSDM*   Short for dynamic systems development method, an agile project delivery framework; for software development projects, DSDM 4 recommends combining its framework with extreme programming; originates from a traditional project management approach and from rapid application development (RAD)

*estimation poker*   Also known as *planning poker*; an estimation technique that leverages the wisdom of crowds; requires each member of a knowledgable group to relatively estimate the effort involved in completing an item with completing other items in the backlog and then collectively share and discuss those individual estimates in order to converge on a group estimate; one way of expressing effort is to use the Fibonacci sequence from 1 up to 21 to ? (where ? means "cannot be estimated")

*extreme programming (XP)*   A software development method consisting of technical and team practices; belongs to the family of agile methods

*future reality tree*   A tool for visualizing the possible outcomes of resolving root causes to problems in a system; one of the thinking processes in the Theory of Constraints

*impediment*   See *blocker*

*incremental*   To increase or add on to something piece by piece; is most useful when the end goal is known and well defined so that value is released with each completed piece *iterative* To create something by repeatedly refining it; is a useful approach when the end goal is unknown or unclear

*kanban* Means "signal board" in Japanese; see also *kanban board*

*kanban (process management)* In lean manufacturing, *kanban* refers to a scheduling system for managing workflow; also known as a kanban system—it was developed by Taiichi Ohno at Toyota in order improve and maintain a high level of production; see also *kanban board*

*Kanban (software development)* Kanban (with an uppercase *K*) usually refers to applying a kanban system to an existing software development life-cycle process—key principles of such a system include visualizing work and limiting work in progress; you create a pull system by applying these principles, which means a team only pulls work in when it has spare capacity

*kanban board* Usually with a lowercase *k*, a kanban board is a tool for visualizing the flow of work and limiting work in progress; see also *work in progress*

*lean manufacturing* A production practice that considers anything that incurs cost and doesn't take you closer to your goal as waste and should therefore be eliminated; also known as *lean enterprise* or *lean production* and sometimes abbreviated to lean

*midsprint review* A meeting that takes place halfway through a sprint during which the whole team shares what has been delivered so far in the current sprint—it is also a chance for the team to reflect on what has happened during the sprint and to identify improvement actions; is not a formal Scrum practice

*minimum viable product (MVP)* The smallest combination of sets of features that form a sufficiently valuable product to the customer

*Perfection Game* A tool for giving feedback that focuses on how to make something perfect through improvement suggestions; one of the core protocols from Jim and Michele McCarthy[2]

*Personal Kanban*   How to use a kanban system to organize your personal life, by Jim Benson and Tonianne DeMaria Barry[3]

*product backlog*   A collection of items for a product, such as user stories—a product backlog can contain items other than user stories; also known as *backlog* in agile

*product backlog refinement*   Referred to as PBR for short; the act of clarifying and refining work items as well as prioritizing them prior to release and sprint planning; usually scheduled as a recurring activity throughout a sprint

*product owner*   Someone responsible for prioritizing and managing the product backlog to maximize the value delivered; usually a business domain expert; a product owner is part of the team

*relative estimation*   A way of estimating items, such as user stories, by comparing the size of one item with another as well as by comparing relatively with the rest of the items in the group; typically used to create a sorted list—one technique for doing relative estimation is *T-shirt sizing*

*release plan*   Consists of a set of goals and a series of sprint backlogs to achieve those goals—this higher-level plan should reflect the underlying value and return on investment (ROI) of items, followed by dependencies, constraints, and risks of the items that make up a release; see also *sprint backlog*

*release planning*   The act of planning goals and work for a release that consist of prioritization and scheduling—a release plan comprises sprint backlogs that make up the release; in agile, the act of planning has a higher value than the plan itself because plans change

---

2.   www.mccarthyshow.com/download-the-core/
3.   www.personalkanban.com/

*retrospective*   A meeting during which one or more people reflect on the past and come up with actions to improve the future; see also *sprint retrospective*

*return on investment (aka ROI)*   A concept that compares investment gains with investment cost—in agile, this is calculated by dividing the estimated value of a requirement with the cost of delivering a corresponding solution

*Scrum*   A process framework for product development and enhancement; based on the three pillars of empirical process control theory: transparency, inspection, and adaptation; includes team and management practices; considered part of the family of agile methods

*Scrum master*   Someone responsible for enabling the team to focus on its work, assisting in the removal of team or organizational blockers; serves as a reminder and guide of the Scrum method, acts as a "servant leader"; depending on the scope of the role, may also be responsible for leading and coaching an organization in using Scrum; see also *agile coach*

*scrum of scrums*   A meeting that requires one representative from each Scrum team to give an update, on behalf of the team, in order to enable multiple teams to synchronize work on a project or across a program; typically follows the format of a daily scrum; see also *daily scrum*

*servant leader*   A leadership style that requires an individual to do whatever is necessary for the team or organization to succeed; requires an individual to know and act according to a set of values that promotes the greater good

*shu-ha-ri*   A concept popularized by the philosophy of aikido that roughly translates to "first learn, then detach, and finally transcend"

*Socratic method*   A tool for critical thinking based on individuals asking and answering questions to challenge the logic behind ideas and beliefs

*sprint*  Used to describe a time box in Scrum ranging from one to four weeks; known as an *iteration* in agile—the recommended sprint length is two weeks for teams new to agile; teams with some experience of Scrum may adapt the sprint length to better suit their context

*sprint backlog*  A list of work items to be delivered for a sprint, usually ordered by taking into consideration the value and return on investment (ROI) of items, followed by dependencies, constraints, and risks

*sprint planning*  The act of planning goals and work for a sprint, consisting of prioritization and planning; a sprint backlog comprises product backlog items and improvement items that make up that sprint's deliverables

*sprint review*  A meeting during which the whole team, including the project stakeholders, come together to look at what has been delivered for that sprint and any work remaining so that it can be taken into account during the planning of the next sprint—it is also an opportunity to reflect on learned or new information from the team and other stakeholders, such as trends and future direction

*sprint retrospective*  A meeting during which the whole team reflects on what happened during the sprint and identifies improvement actions for the future

*story point*  Short for user story point; the unit in which work is estimated—a user story usually has a certain number of story points; see also *relative estimation* and *T-shirt sizing*

*systems thinking*  A process for understanding how parts within a system influence one another and affect the whole

*team*  A group of people who work together toward a common goal and care about one other

*time box*  A fixed period of time—the duration is usually defined up front prior to an activity or work being started

*timeboxing* A simple technique using time boxes to increase focus—if the amount of work planned exceeds that of the time box, it is best practice to replan and start a new time box instead of extending the existing time box to accommodate the work remaining

*T-shirt sizing* A relative estimation technique that sorts items, such as user stories, relative to one another in terms of T-shirt sizes such as S, M, L, XL; see also *relative estimation*

*Tuckman model* Known as Tuckman's group development model; forming, storming, norming, and performing are the phases a group goes through to become an effective team

*user story* Also known as *story*; represents a requirement in agile projects often referred to as a "promise for a conversation"; consists of a goal, the capability, or a feature needed to achieve that goal and the role for which the feature is for; also includes acceptance criteria so that everyone knows when the goal has been achieved—a user story is typically written on an index card (4" x 6") to ensure that it cannot be mistaken as an exhaustive specification of a requirement; described by Bill Wake as "card, conversation, confirmation"

*waterfall (short for waterfall model)* A sequential design process used in software development—the model originates from manufacturing and views progress as steadily flowing downward, like a waterfall, through phases of conception, initiation, analysis, design, construction, testing, production/implementation, and maintenance; agile is considered to be the antithesis of waterfall

*work in progress (WIP)* The amount of work going on at a single point in time—it is common for items to be classified as WIP even though they may be blocked or work has been paused; see also *work-in-progress limit*

*work-in-progress limit (WIP limit)* The maximum number of items to be worked on at any one time; used to ensure a team does not exceed its capacity because that could adversely affect the team's productivity

*value-driven delivery*   A concept that focuses on using the business value of requirements to prioritize and plan

*velocity*   The amount of work completed during a sprint; usually measured by the number of stories completed or the number of story points for completed stories — velocity is useful for progress trending for a team; the general advice is not to compare the velocity between teams for two key reasons: 1) One story point can mean different things to different teams, which prevents a like-for-like or meaningful comparison from being made, and 2) One possible side effect of making such comparisons is that it promotes competition between teams instead of cross-team collaboration

*XP (extreme programming)*   An agile method used for software development that consists of technical and team practices; this method focuses on improving software quality and responsiveness to changing customer requirements

APPENDIX 4

# Bedtime Reading

Here's a list of resources related to the story to help your team with the situations it faces. For sweet dreams, I suggest looking through the resources after a good night's rest and a hearty breakfast.

INTRODUCTION TO AGILE

- *The Scrum Guide* by Jeff Sutherland and Ken Schwaber (16 pages); free download from https://www.scrum.org/Scrum-Guides

- *Scrum and XP from the Trenches* by Henrik Kniberg (130 pages); free download from http://www.infoq.com/minibooks/scrum-xp-from-the-trenches

AGILE

- The Agile Manifesto; available at http://agilemanifesto.org/

- Other resources listed above under Introduction to Agile

LEAN

- *The Toyota Way: 14 Management Principles from the World's Greatest Manufacturer* by Jeffrey Liker

- *Toyota Production System: Beyond Large-Scale Production* by Taiichi Ohno

SCRUM

- Resources listed above under Introduction to Agile

- *Do Better Scrum* by Peter Hundermark; free download from http://www.scrumsense.com/resources/do-better-scrum

KANBAN

- *Priming Kanban* by Jesper Boeg; free download from InfoQ.com

- *Kanban and Scrum: Making the Most of Both* by Henrik Kniberg and Mattias Skarin; free download from InfoQ.com

- *Kanban: Successful Evolutionary Change for Your Technology Business* by David J. Anderson

- *Personal Kanban: Mapping Work/Navigating Life* by Jim Benson and Tonianne DeMaria Barry

EXTREME PROGRAMMING (XP)

- *Extreme Programming Explained: Embrace Change* by Kent Beck with Cynthia Andres

REAL OPTIONS

- "'Real Options' Underlie Agile Practice" by Chris Matts and Olav Maassen; article from InfoQ.com at http://www.infoq.com/articles/real-options-enhance-agility

- *Commitment: A Novel About Managing Projects* by Olav Maassen, Chris Matts, and Chris Geary

REQUIREMENTS

- "Measurable Value with Agile": Value delivery approach by Ryan Shriver; available at http://accu.org/var/uploads/journals/overload89.pdf

- Value Requirements by Tom Gilb; available at http://www.gilb.com/Requirements

- Impact Mapping by Gojko Adzic; available at http://www.impactmapping.org/

- Business Value Modeling by Portia Tung and Pascal Van Cauwenberghe; available at http://www.slideshare.net/agilecoachnet/agreeing-on-business-value

RETROSPECTIVES

- *Agile Retrospective: Making Good Teams Great* by Esther Derby, Diana Larsen, and Ken Schwaber

## PEOPLE AND GROUP DYNAMICS

- *Good to Great* by Jim Collins

- Tuckman's stages of group development (forming, storming, norming, performing), Wikipedia

- *The Wisdom of Crowds* by James Surowiecki

- *The 7 Habits of Highly Effective People* by Stephen R. Covey

## SYSTEMS THINKING

- *The Logical Thinking Process: A Systems Approach to Complex Problem Solving* by H. William Dettmer

- *The Systems Thinking Playbook: Exercises to Stretch and Build Learning and Systems Thinking Capabilities* by Linda Booth Sweeney and Dennis Meadows

APPENDIX 5

# Tools and Exercises Reference

Here's a handy reference to all the tools and exercises that appear in the story so that you can put them to good use.

| NAME | TYPE | WHERE TO FIND IT IN THE BOOK |
|---|---|---|
| The profile card exercise | Ice breaker | *Lighten Up*, on page 237, and *The Profile Card Exercise*, on page 239 |
| Goals definition as a user story | Coaching | *Your Mission*, on page 236 |
| One-on-one conversation plan | Coaching | *Get to Know the Team*, on page 9 |
| One-on-one ice breaker example | Ice breaker | *More About You*, on page 18 |
| Project evaluation | Coaching | *Project Evaluation*, on page 22 |
| Team improvement measures | Coaching | *Measure for Measure*, on page 205 |
| Coach's log | Coaching | *Coach's Log: Day 1*, on page 25 |
| Kanban board | Facilitation | *Agenda*, on page 47, and *Revitalized*, on page 228 |
| Talking token | Facilitation | *Through the Looking Glass*, on page 57 |
| Finger voting for feedback | Facilitation | *Through the Looking Glass*, on page 57 |

| NAME | TYPE | WHERE TO FIND IT IN THE BOOK |
| --- | --- | --- |
| The Perfection Game | Facilitation | *The Perfection Game*, on page 224, and *Group Smarts*, on page 225 |
| Options-based thinking | Planning | *Options, Options, Options*, on page 163 |
| Current reality tree | Systems thinking | *Cause and Effect*, on page 123 |
| Future reality tree | Coaching | *Fortune Telling*, on page 126 |
| Future reality tree with tools | Systems thinking | *Future Reality*, on page 221 |
| Future reality tree with tool descriptions | Systems thinking | *Recommended Tools*, on page 203 |

# Be Agile

Don't just "do" agile; you want to *be* agile. We'll show you how.

The best agile book isn't a book: *Agile in a Flash* is a unique deck of index cards that fit neatly in your pocket. You can tape them to the wall. Spread them out on your project table. Get stains on them over lunch. These cards are meant to be used, not just read.

Jeff Langr and Tim Ottinger
(110 pages) ISBN: 9781934356715. $15
*http://pragprog.com/book/olag*

You know the Agile and Lean development buzzwords, you've read the books. But when systems need a serious overhaul, you need to see how it works in real life, with real situations and people. *Lean from the Trenches* is all about actual practice. Every key point is illustrated with a photo or diagram, and anecdotes bring you inside the project as you discover why and how one organization modernized its workplace in record time.

Henrik Kniberg
(178 pages) ISBN: 9781934356852. $30
*http://pragprog.com/book/hklean*

# Lead Better

So you're the manager. Whether it's one project or a whole portfolio, learn what you need to do to make it work.

This book is a reality-based guide for modern projects. You'll learn how to recognize your project's potholes and ruts, and determine the best way to fix problems—without causing more problems.

And congratulations to Johanna for winning a 2008 Jolt Productivity Award.

Johanna Rothman
(360 pages) ISBN: 9780978739249. $34.95
*http://pragprog.com/book/jrpm*

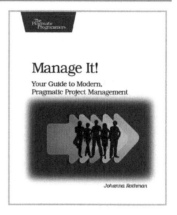

Too many projects? Want to organize them and evaluate them without getting buried under a mountain of statistics? This book will help you collect all your work, decide which projects you should do first, second—and *never*. You'll see how to tie your work to your organization's mission and show your board, your managers, and your staff what you can accomplish and when. You'll get a better view of the work you have, and learn how to make those difficult decisions, ensuring that all your strength is focused where it needs to be.

Johanna Rothman
(210 pages) ISBN: 9781934356296. $32.95
*http://pragprog.com/book/jrport*

# Refactor Your Career

Time to debug and refactor your career, and start doing it right. Start here.

*Technical Blogging* is the first book to specifically teach programmers, technical people, and technically-oriented entrepreneurs how to become successful bloggers. There is no magic to successful blogging; with this book you'll learn the techniques to attract and keep a large audience of loyal, regular readers and leverage this popularity to achieve your goals.

Antonio Cangiano
(288 pages) ISBN: 9781934356883. $33
*http://pragprog.com/book/actb*

You're already a great coder, but awesome coding chops aren't always enough to get you through your toughest projects. You need these 50+ nuggets of wisdom. Veteran programmers: reinvigorate your passion for developing web applications. New programmers: here's the guidance you need to get started. With this book, you'll think about your job in new and enlightened ways.

This title is also available as an audio book.

Ka Wai Cheung
(160 pages) ISBN: 9781934356791. $29
*http://pragprog.com/book/kcdc*

# The Pragmatic Bookshelf

The Pragmatic Bookshelf features books written by developers for developers. The titles continue the well-known Pragmatic Programmer style and continue to garner awards and rave reviews. As development gets more and more difficult, the Pragmatic Programmers will be there with more titles and products to help you stay on top of your game.

# Visit Us Online

### This Book's Home Page
*http://pragprog.com/book/ptdream*
Source code from this book, errata, and other resources. Come give us feedback, too!

### Register for Updates
*http://pragprog.com/updates*
Be notified when updates and new books become available.

### Join the Community
*http://pragprog.com/community*
Read our weblogs, join our online discussions, participate in our mailing list, interact with our wiki, and benefit from the experience of other Pragmatic Programmers.

### New and Noteworthy
*http://pragprog.com/news*
Check out the latest pragmatic developments, new titles and other offerings.

# Save on the eBook

Save on the eBook versions of this title. Owning the paper version of this book entitles you to purchase the electronic versions at a terrific discount.

PDFs are great for carrying around on your laptop—they are hyperlinked, have color, and are fully searchable. Most titles are also available for the iPhone and iPod touch, Amazon Kindle, and other popular e-book readers.

Buy now at *http://pragprog.com/coupon*

# Contact Us

| | |
|---|---|
| Online Orders: | *http://pragprog.com/catalog* |
| Customer Service: | *support@pragprog.com* |
| International Rights: | *translations@pragprog.com* |
| Academic Use: | *academic@pragprog.com* |
| Write for Us: | *http://pragprog.com/write-for-us* |
| Or Call: | +1 800-699-7764 |

CPSIA information can be obtained at www.ICGtesting.com
Printed in the USA
LVOW01s1530180414

382316LV00026B/128/P